THE Prayer Shawl

Journal & GUIDEBOOK

INSPIRATION plus KNIT AND CROCHET BASICS

JANET SEVERI BRISTOW &
VICTORIA A. COLE-GALO

The Taunton Press

TO ALL THE PRAYER SHAWL MAKERS WHO HAVE EMBRACED THE SPIRITUAL
PRACTICE OF CREATING PRAYER SHAWLS, MAY THE WORK OF YOUR HEART
AND HANDS BE BLESSED THREEFOLD. TOGETHER, WE ARE COVERING THE
WORLD IN A SHAWL OF LOVE, COMFORT, AND PEACE.

Text © 2013 by Janet Severi Bristow & Victoria A. Cole-Galo
Photographs © 2013 The Taunton Press, Inc.
Illustrations © 2013 The Taunton Press, Inc.

The Taunton Press
Inspiration for hands-on living®

The Taunton Press, Inc., 63 South Main Street, PO Box 5506, Newtown, CT 06470-5506
e-mail: tp@taunton.com

Editor: Shawna Mullen
Copy editor: Betty Christiansen
Indexer: Cathy Goddard
Jacket, Interior, and Layout design: Rita Sowins / Sowins Design
Illustrators: Christopher Clapp p. 12; Christine Erikson pp. 9, 139, 140, 141; Carol Ruzicka pp. 10, 11
Photographers: Zach DeSart pp. 2, 3, 85, 86, 93, 94, 97, 138, 139, 140, 149; Tina Hilton p. 19;
Tom Hopkins pp. cover (shawl), 5, 82, 98, 101, 139, 141; Jeff McNamara pp. 103, 104, 106, 109, 110, 113;
Scott Phillips pp. 35, 38, 42, 46, 50, 54, 58, 63, 66, 71, 74, 78

The following names/manufacturers appearing in *The Prayer Shawl Journal & Guidebook* are trademarks:
Bernat®, Caron® Perfect Match, Caron® Simply Soft, Jo-Ann™ Sensations™, Lion Brand® Vanna's Choice®,
Louet™, Plymouth Yarn®, Rosarios4®

Library of Congress Cataloging-in-Publication Data
Bristow, Janet.
  The prayer shawl journal and guidebook : inspiration, plus knit & crochet basics / Janet Severi Bristow, Victoria A. Cole-Galo.
    pages cm.
  ISBN 978-1-62113-673-6 (pbk.)
1. Knitting--Patterns. 2. Shawls. 3. Religion in art. I. Cole-Galo, Victoria A.. II. Title.
TT825.B742 2013
746.43'2--dc23
                        2013036232

Printed in the United States of America
10 9 8 7 6 5 4 3 2 1

Acknowledgments

Once again, The Taunton Press has given us the opportunity to create a book in the Prayer Shawl series. Many thanks to executive editor Shawna Mullen, editor Renee Neiger, copy editor Betty Christiansen, and the book group at Taunton. The entire team has done a wonderful job of putting together a beautiful and unique publication. We are pleased and most grateful to all of you!

From Janet: With gratitude and appreciation to Vicky, with whom I have shared this unexpected journey of Spirit and Sisterhood, may we always remember the gifts and blessings this ministry has brought into our lives. To every person who has picked up needles or hook to craft a shawl as a gesture of love and concern, thank you! We are all members of a global family based on love and prayer, offering comfort one stitch at a time. You are a blessing to me and the world. And to my family, your love and support enables me to reach out far beyond what I could have ever imagined!

And last, but most important, we are humbled, honored, and grateful to our Creator, in whose hands this ministry lies.

From Vicky: All my love and gratitude to my husband, Zeke, and to our sons, Jonathan and Nick. Special thanks to my parents, Gladys and Fran, to my mother-in-law, Rita, to my family and friends, and to Janet—who has walked this path in sisterhood with me—you have blessed my life in so many ways, I am grateful!

Contents

How to Use This Journal

We are pleased to bring you *The Prayer Shawl Journal &
Guidebook*. We designed this book for you, whether you are
a beginner making your first prayer shawl or an established
"prayer shawler" seeking a more comprehensive experience.

We have included simple knit and crochet instructions and steps to follow through
the shawl-making process. In these pages, you will find instructions for basic stitches and
techniques, a chart to help you choose proper-sized knitting needles and crochet hooks,
information on reading knitting and crochet abbreviations, and tips for how to achieve
the correct gauge.

Designed to be interactive with the user, both The Prayer Shawl Year and Stitch
Along chapters offer places for you to keep project notes, track your tools (such as needles
and hooks), and take inventory of your yarn stash.

To help you complete your shawl, handy tips and ideas are included for adding
finishing touches such as fringe, tassels, a macramé edging, and a simple crocheted edge.
Guidance is given for personalizing the shawl for the recipient by adding beads, charms,
and medals. These embellishments not only add beauty, but can also provide a source of
meditation and reflection for the shawl recipient. Finally, we've offered examples of our
favorite ways to present a shawl, which include instructions on how to make a potpourri/
essential oil sachet and two examples of custom-made Prayer Shawl Gift Bags.

The Journaling Experience

The Prayer Shawl Year chapter is divided into the 12 months of the calendar year. Months are paired with favorite knit and crochet stitches for you to try; once you feel confident using them, refer to the multiples technique on p. 31 to incorporate them into shawl designs of your own.

Prayer shawl making is a spiritual practice based in prayer and good intentions for the recipient, so we left room in The Prayer Shawl Year chapter for you to keep a journal and take the shawl-making experience to a deeper level. Within each month, you will find inspirational quotes, reflective journaling prompts, and space to write. Your writings can be a wonderful starting point for poems, prayers, and blessings to accompany the shawls you give, if you wish.

Scattered among the pages like little blessings are ideas for enhancing your prayer shawls with symbolic colors, beads, charms, and fragrances. Also included are suggestions for creating the setting for peaceful and reflective shawl making, incorporating quiet music, candles, and suggested teas to sip for relaxation. As you can see, the entire prayer shawl-making process becomes a sensory experience from start to finish:

- the texture, warmth, and color of the yarn
- the sparkle of the beads and charms
- music, prayer, and good thoughts to calm the spirit
- the scent of a candle or sachet
- the taste of a relaxing cup of tea in your favorite mug

You might go even further by sharing your musings and inspirations with your prayer shawl recipient in a note. Also consider including the title of the music you played and perhaps a sachet scented with the same aroma of the candle you lit while making the shawl.

We invite you to carve out some time for yourself, find a quiet space, and take a few deep breaths. Pull out your knitting or crocheting, select your favorite pen and journal, pour yourself a cup of tea, light a candle, and turn on inspirational music. As you settle in and embrace your knitting or crocheting—the work of your hands—you also embrace the receiver of your shawl. With every stitch that you create, may your heart be joyful.

PEACE,
JANET & VICKY

The Basics

Casting On

LONG-TAIL CAST-ON

The long-tail cast-on, also known as the half-hitch cast-on, is probably the most frequently used method for placing knitting stitches on the needle. It's popular because it's easy to execute and results in a neat, elastic edge.

1. To begin, leave a long end of yarn that's about four times the length of the edge to be cast on, and make a slip knot, as shown above. Place it on a needle in your right hand, with the short end hanging near you.

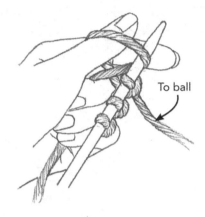

2. With the left hand, hold the short end under the last three fingers and make a loop on the left thumb. Insert the needle through the loop as shown.

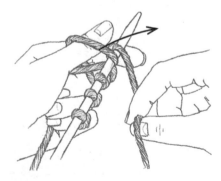

3. With the right hand, wrap the yarn from the ball around the needle tip from left to right and lift the thumb loop over the needle tip to form a new stitch.

TECHNIQUE

KNITTED CAST-ON: The knitted cast-on allows you to put simple knit stitches (see p. 10) onto the needle. Knit 1 stitch without removing the original stitch from the left needle. Transfer the new stitch back onto the left needle by slipping it "knitwise." Continue in this manner, always making the new stitch into the one just transferred to the left needle.

CABLE CAST-ON

If you cast on using the cable method, your cast-on edge will be nice and firm.

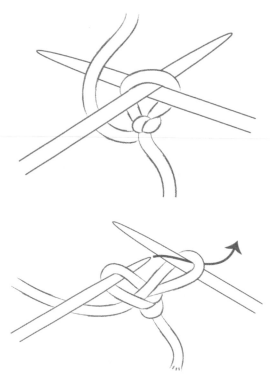

2. Next, insert the right needle between the first 2 stitches on the left needle, as shown. Draw through a loop and transfer it to the left needle. Repeat for the required number of stitches.

I. For the cable cast-on, you need 2 stitches on the needle to begin, so make one by placing a slip knot on the left needle; make the second by knitting into the first and transferring the new stitch to the left needle. Insert the right needle tip into the loop, knit a stitch, and place it on the left needle (as with the Knitted Cast-On on the facing page).

TECHNIQUE

I-CORD: The I-cord is a simple cord or tie you can knit. Using double-pointed needles, cast on the required number of stitches (usually 4 or 5); the working yarn will be on the left side of the needle. *Hold the needle with the stitches in your left hand, bring the yarn around behind the stitches to the right side, and knit stitches from right to left, pulling the yarn tightly behind the work when knitting the first stitch. Do not turn. Repeat from * until the cord is the desired length.

The Knit Stitch

Garter stitch is the most popular (and easiest) knitting stitch: Simply knit all rows. If you are new to knitting (or just rusty) remember that you should never knit directly from the skein of yarn. You must first wind any yarn that comes in a skein into a ball (page 18). Although it seems faster to knit from the skein, you risk disaster because skeins have a way of becoming a tangled mess as knitting progresses.

1. To make the knit stitch, make sure the yarn is in back of your work, then insert the point of the right needle into the first stitch on the left needle from front to back and push it through until the point of the right needle is behind the left needle.

2. Wrap the yarn around the back of the right needle, then between the two needle points, toward your right hand.

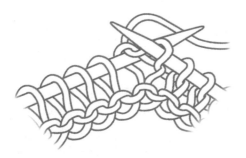

3. Bring the wrap back through the stitch on the left needle to form a new stitch on the right needle.

4. Drop the stitch off the left needle.

The Purl Stitch

A row of purl stitches, alternated with a row of knit stitches, creates stockinette stitch. In stockinette, you knit the right-side (RS) rows and purl the wrong-side (WS) rows.

TECHNIQUE

SEED STITCH: To create a seed stitch design, knit 1, purl 1 across the row. For all subsequent rows, knit the purl stitches and purl the knit stitches as they face you.

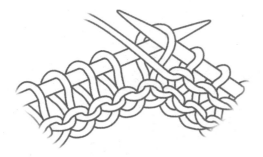

I. With the yarn in front of your work, insert the point of the right needle into the first stitch on the left needle from back to front. The right needle should be in front of the left needle, as shown.

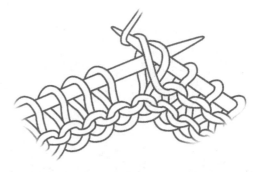

2. Wrap the yarn around the right needle between the needles first, then around to the front of the right needle and back toward the right.

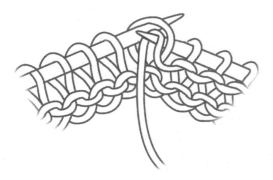

3. Pull the wrap back through the loop on the left needle, forming a new stitch on the right needle.

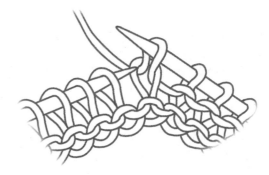

4. Drop the stitch from the left needle.

Left-Handed Knitting

A left handed person can knit just as easily as a right-handed one: No matter which hand is dominant, knitters use both hands (thanks to the fact that there are two needles), and left-handed people can learn to knit "right-handed." However, if you prefer a little left-tailored instruction, try out the following method.

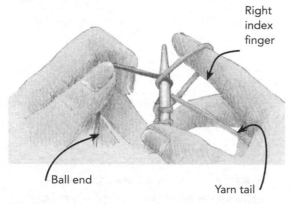

Right index finger

Ball end

Yarn tail

I. Cast on by holding the ball end of the yarn in your left hand and the yarn tail in your right, scoop a loop with the right index finger and slip it onto the needle. Carry the ball end across the needle from right to left and lift the loop over it and off the needle.

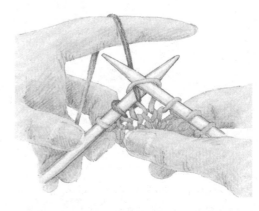

2. Make a knit stitch by inserting the left needle from front to back through the first stitch on the right needle. Wrap yarn from under needle, over the top, and away; pull wrap through loop.

TECHNIQUE

If you are a "right-knitting lefty," be aware that knitting patterns have a right-handed bias and you may face some subtle problems. Cables are the biggest challenge, as stitches can end up twisting backward. This shouldn't be a barrier to trying more difficult patterns, just good to be aware.

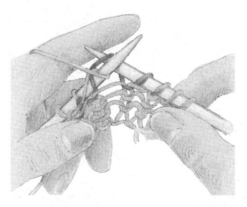

3. Purl by inserting the left needle from back to front of the first stitch on the right needle. Wrap yarn from over needle and pull wrap through loop.

Left-Handed Increasing, Decreasing, and Slip Stitch

A left-handed person can knit just as easily as a right-handed one; here is a little left-tailored instruction to show you how.

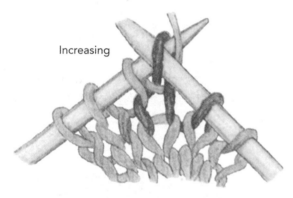

Increasing

1. Increase by knitting into the stitch, but don't remove the old loop. Insert the left needle into the back of the loop and knit a second stitch into it (kf&b).

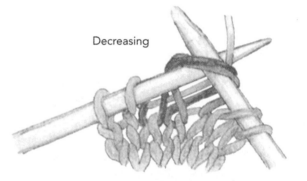

Decreasing

2. To decrease, or knit two together (k2tog), insert the left needle into 2 stitches, second stitch first, and knit them together as 1 stitch—the decrease will slant to the left.

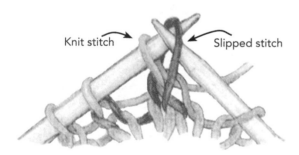

Knit stitch   Slipped stitch

3. A right-slanting decrease is made with a stitch sequence in which you slip 1, knit 1, and pass the slipped stitch over—abbreviated as (skp) in knitting patterns. For the left-handed version, slip the first stitch to the left needle without knitting it; knit the next stitch. Using the right needle, lift the slipped stitch over the knit stitch and off the needle.

Slipping a Stitch and Increasing

Slipping a stitch (purlwise)—abbreviated as (sl 1 pwise) in knitting patterns—is a way to move a stitch to the right needle without knitting it.

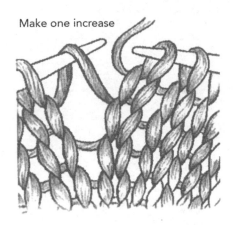

Make one increase

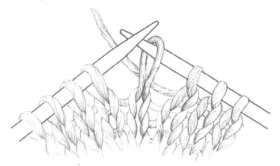

I. On right-side rows, with the yarn in back, insert the right needle as if to purl (see p. 11), slipping the stitch in this position onto the right needle. On wrong-side rows, do the same, except with the yarn in front. Be careful not to insert the right needle as if you were going to knit—the slipped stitch will end up twisted instead of lying flat.

I. To make one, or increase by 1 stitch, first lift the strand of yarn running between the stitches on the right and left needle from front to back.

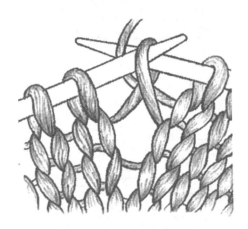

2. Next, knit or purl the new stitch in the back, as shown. You will notice that the make one stitch is twisted, which prevents a hole from forming below it in the next row.

TECHNIQUE

MAKE ONE: Make one is an easy way to add a stitch and increase the width of your knitted piece. This stitch is abbreviated as (m1) in knitting patterns.

Decreasing

There are several ways to decrease stitches. Among the most common are slip, slip, knit—abbreviated (ssk) in knitting patterns—and knit two together, which is abbreviated (k2tog). Worked on the knit side of the fabric, the ssk decrease slants to the left, while the k2tog slants to the right.

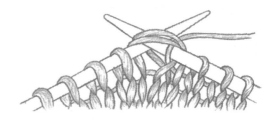

2. Knit two together (k2tog). Insert the right needle as if to knit (knitwise) through 2 stitches at once and knit them together as if they were 1 stitch.

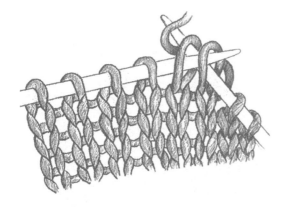

1. Slip, slip, knit (ssk). Slip 2 stitches, one at a time, as if to knit. Insert the left needle into these stitches from left to right, as shown, and knit them together.

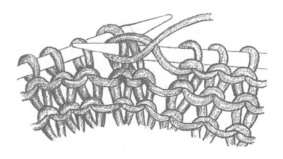

3. To decrease on a purl row, purl two together (p2tog) through the back loops, as follows: Insert the tip of the right needle into the back of the next 2 purl stitches on the left needle, second stitch first, then wrap the yarn and purl them as 1 stitch.

TECHNIQUE

MATTRESS STITCH: This is a seaming technique that joins two pieces of stockinette stitch (see p. 11). It is done in the space between the edge stitch (selvage stitch) and the stitch next to it. Lay the pieces to be joined side by side with the right side facing you. Pull the edge stitch slightly away from the stitch next to it, and insert your needle under the horizontal bar on the opposite piece. Work back and forth, inserting the needle under the bar on one piece and then the other until you have worked a few rows. Pull the yarn in the direction of the seam so the two rows come together and abut one another. Continue until you complete the seam.

Three Ways to Bind Off

The most popular method for binding off or casting off knit and purl stitches is a basic bind-off in which you chain the stitches off the right needle one at a time. If the yarn is heavy or irregular, choose the quick bind-off method shown below in 2. The stranded bind-off (3) is another very easy way to bind off your work.

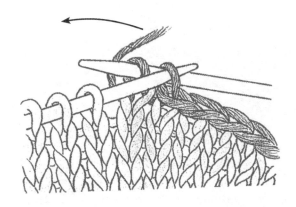

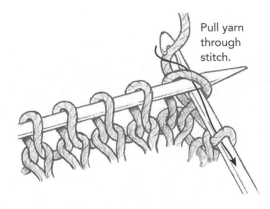

Pull yarn through stitch.

I. For the basic bind-off, first work 2 stitches, in either knitting or purling to match the stitches in the row below. Then insert the left needle from left to right into the right stitch on the right needle, lift this stitch over the left stitch, and drop the right stitch off the needle. Knit or purl another stitch from the left needle, and repeat the process with the 2 stitches on the right needle, as shown. Repeat across the row. When there is 1 stitch remaining, cut the yarn, leaving the end long if it's necessary for sewing, and pull the end through the remaining stitch.

2. For a quick bind-off using heavy yarn on a bulky garment, substitute a crochet hook approximately the same diameter as the knitting needle. Put the hook through the first loop on the left needle and knit the stitch onto the hook. Knit the next stitch onto the hook and pull the new stitch through the first one, as shown. Continue in this manner to the end of the row and pull the yarn through the last loop on the hook.

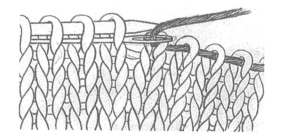

3. The stranded bind-off is a great method for securing stitches when your project is complete. Cut the yarn end about a foot longer than the width of the knitting and thread a blunt tapestry needle. Beginning at the side that has the yarn end, slip the tapestry needle through several stitches on the knitting needle, as shown; pull the yarn through, then drop the stitches off the knitting needle. Repeat across the row.

TECHNIQUE

STAY LOOSE: There are dozens of ways to bind off in knitting—though most are for creating a decorative edge. The key thing to remember about binding off is to concentrate on binding off loosely: if your bind-off is too tight, you could end up with an edge that puckers or ruffles.

"In through the front door,
once around the back,
peek through the window,
and off jumps Jack."

—TRADITIONAL RHYME ON LEARNING TO KNIT

Winding Yarn, Joining a New Color, Gauge Swatches

Here are few helpful tricks that will smooth your path as you knit. The first is a simple way to wind yarn into a foolproof yarn ball that pulls from the center without tangling; next, joining a new color of yarn to create stripes or a pretty contrast; last, making gauge swatches—an essential start to all projects.

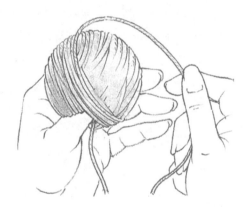

I. To make a foolproof center-pull ball, start with a small plastic medicine bottle. Place the end of the yarn inside the bottle and snap the cap shut. Wind the yarn loosely around the bottle. When finished, remove the bottle and release the yarn end. If you wind the yarn uniformly, you'll finish with a neat, slightly flat ball that pulls easily from the center and won't roll away.

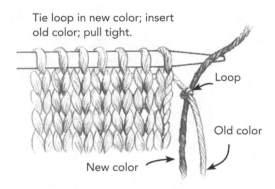

Tie loop in new color; insert old color; pull tight.

Loop

Old color

New color

2. Joining a new yarn color is easy. Begin by tying a loop in the new yarn. Slip the old yarn through the loop, pull the new yarn firmly up against the edge of the swatch, then tie a square knot with the two ends. The square knot will prevent the ends from slipping, even if the yarn is fine or slippery. Continue knitting with the new color, and weave the ends into the back side of your project.

3. All knitting begins with a gauge swatch, because gauge—getting the correct number of stitches and rows to the inch—is critical to success. To check your gauge, knit at least a 4-in. square in the stitch pattern and needles your pattern calls for, and bind it off. Lay the swatch on a flat surface and carefully measure the number of stitches and rows per inch (most patterns give you the number of stitches and rows you will get over 4 in.). Compare the numbers you get to the gauge given in your pattern. If you are getting *more* stitches/rows per inch than your pattern calls for, it means your stitches are too small, and you should change to the next larger needle. If you are getting *fewer* stitches/rows per inch, your stitches are too large, and you should try the next smaller needle. Change needle sizes until your gauge matches that given in the pattern.

Knitting Abbreviations

approx	approximate(ly)		oz	ounce(s)
BO	bind off		p	purl
CC	contrasting color		psso	pass slipped stitch over decrease
ch	chain (crochet)		p2tog	purl 2 stitches together (decrease)
CO	cast on		RS	right side
dc	double crochet		sc	single crochet
dec	decrease		sk	skip (crochet)
k	knit		sl	slip
K1-b	knit 1 stitch through the back loop		ssk	slip 1 stitch knitwise, slip 1 stitch knitwise, knit the 2 slipped stitches together (decrease)
Kf&b	knit in the front and back of 1 stitch (increase)			
K2tog	knit 2 stitches together		st/sts	stitch/stitches
in	inch(es)		tog	together
inc	increase		WS	wrong side
MC	main color		yd	yard(s)
m1	make 1 stitch (increase)		yo	yarn over

Crochet Abbreviations*

beg	beginning		rep	repeat	
CC	contrasting color		rev sc or crab st	reverse single crochet	
ch	chain		rnd	round	
dc	double crochet		RS	right side	
dc2tog	double crochet 2 together, a decrease		sc	single crochet	
dec	decrease		sc2tog	single crochet 2 together, a decrease	
FPdc	front post double crochet		sk	skip	
FPtr	front post treble crochet		sl st	slip stitch	
g	gram		t-ch or tch	turning chain	
hdc	half-double crochet		tog	together	
inc	increase		tr	treble crochet	
MC	main color		WS	wrong side	
mm	millimeters		yo	yarn over	
oz	ounce				

* The master list for the Craft Yarn Council of America is available at http://www.craftyarncouncil.com/crochet.html

"I pray that each stitch may forever keep my prayers for you and for your well-being."

—IRMA LANDESFEIND

The Crochet Stitch

A slip knot and chain are the basis of all crochet. Basic stitches include single crochet, a two-step stitch that makes a firm, nonstretchy fabric, and half-double crochet, which produces a slightly taller stitch than single crochet. (For more crochet stitches, see p. 22.)

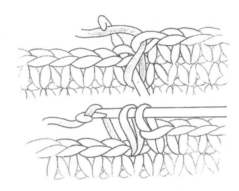

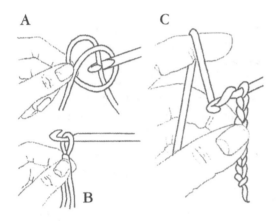

I. To create a crochet foundation chain of stitches, make a slip knot by forming a loop and pulling the yarn from behind the loop through to the front with the crochet hook (drawing A); tighten gently (drawing B). Make a chain by wrapping the yarn over the hook (yo), and pulling the hook and yarn through the loop (drawing C); tighten and repeat.

2. To continue working in single crochet (sc), insert the hook from front to back through both loops of the stitch below. Yarn over and pull up a loop; you now have 2 loops on the hook. Yarn over again, and pull through both loops.

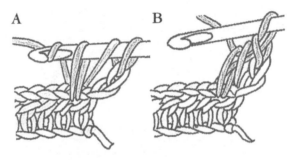

3. To continue working in half-double crochet (hdc), yarn over and insert the hook into the work; yarn over and pull up a loop (drawing A). Yarn over and pull through all 3 loops on the hook (drawing B).

TECHNIQUE

TRICKY FIRST ROW New to crochet and finding the first row tricky? Ask someone more experienced to start a few starting rows—then, pick up the piece and keep crocheting. The work will be easier to hold, and, once you have worked enough rows, it will be easier to begin the next time.

Double, Triple, and Crab-Stitch Crochet

Double crochet creates a tall stitch, and it works up more quickly than single crochet. Triple crochet stitches are still taller, and the resulting fabric is thick. Crab-stitch crochet, also called backward crochet, produces a beautiful corded edging.

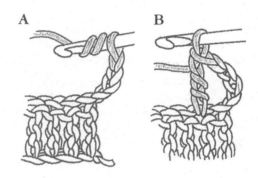

2. For treble or triple crochet (tr), work as follows: Yarn over twice (drawing A); insert hook into work. Yarn over and pull up a loop; yarn over again and pull through first 2 loops only. Yarn over and pull through next 2 loops; yarn over and pull through the last 2 loops on the hook (drawing B shows the completed stitch).

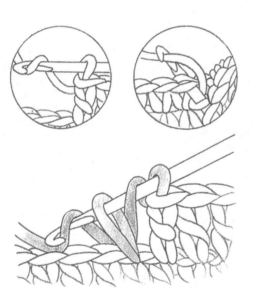

1. For double crochet (dc), work as follows: Yarn over, insert the hook through the loops as for single crochet, then yarn over and pull up a loop; you now have 3 loops on the hook, as shown. Yarn over and pull through 2 of the loops, then yarn over again and pull through the remaining 2 loops on the hook.

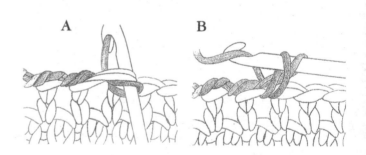

3. Crab-stitch crochet is worked almost like single crochet, except from left to right. Work a row of single crochet from right to left, as usual. Do not turn the work. Chain 1, *insert the hook under the next stitch to the right, pick up the yarn by dropping the head of the hook over it, and draw up a long loop (drawing A). Wrap yarn over the hook and pull through both loops on the hook (drawing B).* Repeat from * to *.

Crochet Increases and Decreases

Increasing in crochet—abbreviated (inc) in crochet patterns—is when 2 stitches are crocheted in 1 stitch. Working a decrease (dec) narrows the crochet fabric by eliminating a stitch.

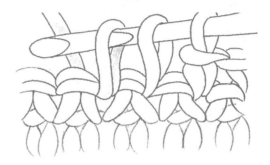

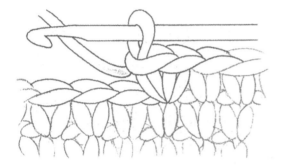

I. To increase in single or double crochet, crochet 2 stitches in 1 stitch, as shown.

TECHNIQUE

WORKING INTO THE FRONT OR BACK LOOP:
Crochet is usually worked into both the front and back loops at the top of a stitch in the row below, with the hook inserted from front to back. If you insert the hook in the front loop only, the other stitch becomes a horizontal bar that can be an interesting pattern.

2. To decrease in single crochet, start by pulling up a loop as usual. Now insert the hook into the following stitch, yarn over, and pull up a loop (shown); yarn over and pull yarn through all 3 loops on the hook.

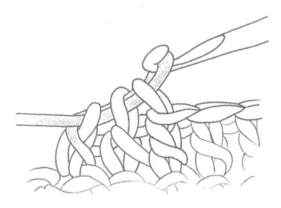

3. To decrease in double crochet, start by working a stitch as usual; stop at the last step when there are 2 loops left on the hook. Yarn over, insert the hook into the following stitch and pull up a loop, yarn over and pull through 2 loops, then yarn over and pull through the remaining 3 loops on the hook, as shown.

Standard Yarn Weights

YARN	NUMBERED BALL	DESCRIPTION	STS/4 IN.	NEEDLE SIZE / CROCHET HOOK SIZE
SUPERFINE	1	Sock, baby, fingering	27–32	U.S. 1–3 / B–1 to E–4
FINE	2	Sport, baby	23–26	U.S. 3–5 / E–4 to 7
LIGHT	3	DK, light worsted	21–24	U.S. 5–7 / 7 to I–9
MEDIUM	4	Worsted, afghan, Aran	16–20	U.S. 7–9 / I–9 to K–10½
BULKY	5	Chunky, craft, rug	12–15	U.S. 9–11 / K–10½ to M–13
SUPER BULKY	6	Bulky, roving	6–11	U.S. 11 and larger / M–13 and larger

"One single grateful thought raised to heaven is the most perfect prayer."

—G.E. LESSING

Metric Equivalency Chart

One inch equals approximately 2.54 centimeters. To convert inches to centimeters, multiply the figure in inches by 2.54 and round off to the nearest half centimeter, or use the chart below, whose figures are rounded off (1 centimeter equals 10 millimeters).

⅛ in. = 3 mm	9 in. = 23 cm
¼ in. = 6 mm	10 in. = 25.5 cm
⅜ in. = 1 cm	12 in. = 30.5 cm
½ in. = 1.3 cm	14 in. = 35.5 cm
⅝ in. = 1.5 cm	15 in. = 38 cm
¾ in. = 2 cm	16 in. = 40.5 cm
⅞ in. = 2.2 cm	18 in. = 45.5 cm
1 in. = 2.5 cm	20 in. = 51 cm
2 in. = 5 cm	21 in. = 53.5 cm
3 in. = 7.5 cm	22 in. = 56 cm
4 in. = 10 cm	24 in. = 61 cm
5 in. = 12.5 cm	25 in. = 63.5 cm
6 in. = 15 cm	36 in. = 92 cm
7 in. = 18 cm	45 in. = 63.5 cm
8 in. = 20.5 cm	60 in. = 152 cm

Crochet Hook Sizes

MILLIMETER RANGE	U.S. SIZE RANGE
2.25 mm	B-1
2.75 mm	C-2
3.25 mm	D-3
3.5 mm	E-4
3.75 mm	F-5
4 mm	G-6
4.5 mm	7
5 mm	H-8
5.5 mm	I-9
6 mm	J-10
6.5 mm	K-10½
8 mm	L-11
9 mm	M/N-13
10 mm	N/P-15
15 mm	P/Q
16 mm	Q
19 mm	S

The Prayer Shawl Year

JANUARY TO DECEMBER

Starting a Prayer Shawl
Journal

Now that you have become more comfortable and learned some basic techniques of knitting and crocheting, just as important is the thoughtful process that goes into creating a prayer shawl. Prayer Shawl making is about putting your heart into your work. It is an opportunity to take time out of your busy day or week, to sit and create something beautiful that will bring comfort or happiness to another person.

SETTING THE INTENTION

Most often, we knit or crochet on the run, grabbing bits of time during our busy schedules. It's important to create a space for yourself especially when beginning a new shawl. When you do, it sets your intention of beginning the spiritual practice of shawl making. A small ritual of brewing a lovely cup of tea, lighting a special candle, and playing soft music sets the stage for what you are about to do.

COMBINING PRAYER SHAWL MAKING AND JOURNALING

This chapter is segmented into 12 calendar months: Each month offers a quote followed by questions we hope will inspire you to write a reflection. Keeping your journal at hand with your supplies will help you to capture thoughts, ideas, and inspirations as you knit or crochet. Be sure to include the date you start a new shawl, your reasons for selecting the yarn, and any other tidbits you'd like to include. Keep a listening heart and record what you "hear." Saying a prayer or poem or reading an inspirational passage declares that you care about the recipient, even if you don't know who will receive the shawl. Most often, we know who the shawl is for by the time we're finished. If not, don't worry. When the time comes, it'll go to the person meant to receive it. For you, the shawl maker, adding little pieces of yarn, sketches, doodles, or photos to the pages of this journal captures your unique personality, making this your own one-of-a kind book! As you build your journal, you'll see the wonder of how each shawl you make weaves a story. Looking back over these pages is a great way to remember the shawls you've designed and the people you gave them to. When you do, it is another opportunity to send them more good thoughts and blessings!

For each month, we also include a knit/crochet stitch pattern or motif. If you're uncertain about a pattern and before you invest in larger amounts of yarn for a prayer shawl, try making a swatch out of leftover yarn from your stash. Smaller swatches can be made into a prayer cloth or scarf. Some shawl makers will include smaller items such as these with the shawls they give for use by family members. This not only offers comfort, but also helps to unite the family in difficult times.

ENCOMPASSING THE SENSES—SIGHT, AROMA, TEXTURE

If you know the recipient, selecting her or his favorite color for the shawl is a good choice. But experimenting with the symbolism of different colors can add depth of meaning to the shawl. The color of the yarn can convey your sentiments, such as pink for love and friendship, or blue for tranquility and peace. The color theme also can be carried throughout your prayer shawl making when lighting a candle or adding colored beads to the finished shawl.

When completing your shawl, the final prayer and thoughts can be just as important as the starting ones. Here you'll have an opportunity to add further intentions and prayers into the piece. Even tying and knotting the fringe or tassels is an opportunity for keeping a prayerful intention with each strand. We've heard from one prayer shawl maker that she says a final blessing over her shawls to remove any frustrations she may have thought or spoken throughout the prayer shawl-making process. Lay your hand on the shawl in your lap and offer up a final wish or blessing before giving it away. Include that blessing with the shawl, if you'd like. Don't forget to say a little prayer for yourself.

Once the shawl is finished, how it is presented can help extend the beauty and meaning of the gift. Those final touches or embellishments convey just as much sentiment as the shawl itself. Shawls can be wrapped up in tissue paper or cloth and placed into gift bags or boxes. On p. 142 we have provided you with instructions for making two types of presentation bags. One is created from fabric and the other is either knitted or crocheted.

FINISHING TOUCHES

It's a blessing to be able to present a shawl to someone. It can be a tender moment for both and a moment to remember. In fact, the perfect, full-circle conclusion to your journaling experience for the shawl, is to record a postscript entry about the presentation. Your reaction is just as important as the recipient's.

At this point in preparing the gift, you will also want to decide which items to include with your shawl such as a potpourri or essential oil sachet (see p. 142). If you add beads or charms, it's nice to include a description of their symbolism and why you chose to include them. It is helpful for the recipient to have an explanation of what a prayer shawl is. Providing this insight helps with understanding the meaning behind the shawl and your purpose or intentions for making the gift. Don't be surprised if someday, the person to whom you gave the shawl asks you to teach her to become a shawl maker, too!

This is also the time to look back upon your journal and read through your thoughts and ponderings. You can include these thoughts in a personal note, or try your hand at turning them into a poem or prayer. Sometimes even a simple quote from a poem or scripture verse can convey your sentiments to the recipient. To enable the recipient to have a sensory experience when receiving the shawl, as you did when beginning to create the shawl, you could include a colored candle, scented sachet, and a CD of music you listened to while working on the shawl. Other options to add are a box of flavored tea, some hand cream, or a journal and pen.

Our hope for you is that you will continue to see journaling as an essential part of your prayer shawl-making experience, and that you continue to be inspired by wisdom and the insights learned as you embrace your spiritual practice.

If you've never kept a journal, it might take a while to get used to recording your thoughts. Once you're comfortable with the process, you might be surprised rereading the quiet thoughts you captured while in a meditative space. We have heard from many prayer shawl makers that they believe they receive more benefits than the recipient. That's because as the shawl maker gives away shawls, blessings circle back to her which encourages the making of another shawl . . . and so on and so on. May that grace fill you with the same desire!

STITCH OF THE MONTH

To those who are new to the art of making prayer shawls, we have given you a stitch of the month to play with.

The instructions start with the "multiples" of each stitch needed to create a pattern. This means that you cast on or chain a multiple of the number provided. A multiple of 3 would be any number that is divisible by 3. Then, if the directions continue by saying "plus 1," that means you only add 1 stitch that one time. So, for instance, if the directions say to work in multiples of 3 plus 1 stitch, you would pick a number divisible by 3, then add 1 and cast on or chain that number of stitches.

At first, it's advisable to work up little swatches with different types of yarn using various yarn weights and needle/hook sizes to see how you like the look of the stitch. You can also use the hook and needle size recommended on the yarn label. These swatches can be kept together to inspire you. Make sure the sample has a tag on which is written the details (the type, brand, color, and, if known, the lot number), and weight of the yarn, as well as the size of the needle or hook you used.

January

"Winter, a lingering season, is a time to gather golden moments, embark upon a sentimental journey, and enjoy every idle hour."
—JOHN BOSWELL

COLOR: Burgundy—Memory, Truth, Comfort

GEMSTONES: Garnet—Faithfulness
Rose Quartz—Unconditional Love

FLOWER: Carnation—Joy

TEA: Chai Latte

MUSIC TO STITCH BY: "Dance of the Blessed Spirits" from *Orpheus and Eurydice* by Christoph Gluck

SCENT: White Ginger

SYMBOLS: Snowflake, Snowdrop

THOUGHTS TO JOURNAL

Most of us don't have the luxury of
enjoying idle hours. Take some time
this month to enjoy a quiet hour
or two of knitting or crocheting.
Weave some golden threads among
your work in hand as a symbol
of this golden time. Record your
thoughts and feelings. Perhaps a
poem or a blessing might form as
you write.

January

KNIT STITCH OF THE MONTH:
Rice Stitch

Cast on a multiple of 2 + 1.
ROW ONE: P1, (k1 through the back loop, p1) across.
ROW TWO: Knit all sts.
Rep these 2 rows for pattern.

February

"When we visited, we prayed and wrapped ourselves in our prayer shawls, their fringes tangling together as we held hands."
—GLADYS COLE

COLOR: Pink—Compassion, Sensitivity, Generosity

GEMSTONES: Amethyst—Sincerity
Onyx—Relaxation

FLOWER: Violet—Spirituality

TEA: Jasmine

MUSIC TO STITCH BY: "Jesu, Joy of Man's Desiring" by Johann Sebastian Bach

SCENT: Lavender

SYMBOLS: Heart, Flower

THOUGHTS TO JOURNAL

Think about a time when you've
knit or crocheted with a friend
or presented a shawl to someone
close. Take some time to reflect
on your experience: What
feelings or thoughts are evoked?
You may even want to share
your thoughts with your friend!

February

CROCHET STITCH OF THE MONTH:
Heart Stitch

Chain a multiple of 5 + 2.
ROW ONE: Turn. Ch 2. Sk 3 ch of base ch,*
in next ch (2 dc, ch 1, 2 dc),
sk 4 ch*.
Rep from * to * across, ending with dc
in last ch.
ROW TWO: Turn. Ch 2. Sk 3 dc *over ch-1
(2 dc, ch 1, 2 dc), sk 4 dc*.
Rep from * to * across, ending with sk 2 dc,
dc in tch.
Rep Row Two for pattern.

March

"We cannot live for ourselves alone.
Our lives are connected by a thousand
invisible threads, and along these
sympathetic fibers, our actions run as
causes and return to us as results."
—HERMAN MELVILLE

COLOR: Green—Growth, Healing, Prosperity

GEMSTONES: Aquamarine—Calm, Protection
Bloodstone—Courage

FLOWER: Daffodil—Regard, Chivalry

TEA: Irish Breakfast

MUSIC TO STITCH BY: "Air" from the Orchestral
Suite No. 3 by Johann Sebastian Bach

SCENT: Clary Sage

SYMBOL: Shamrock

THOUGHTS TO JOURNAL

As you create a prayer shawl, imagine that each stitch, each row, is a visible thread of sympathetic feeling that reaches out to others and circles back to you. As you give compassion, you are filled with more compassion and so on, with each shawl. Has your connection to others changed since you've been creating prayer shawls? Has participating in this ministry revealed any different insights regarding compassion for others?

Wrap yourself in a completed shawl, and feel the effects of your own loving concern.

March

_____

_____

_____

_____

_____

_____

_____

_____

_____

_____

_____

CROCHET STITCH OF THE MONTH:
Trinity Stitch

Chain a multiple of 2 +3.
ROW ONE: Turn. Ch 2, sk tch, *over 3 ch
sc3tog, ch 1*, insert hook in same ch as
previous sc and rep from * to * across,
ending with sc in last st.
ROW TWO: Ch 2, Beginning in ch, *over
(ch, sc3tog, ch) sc3tog, ch 1*, insert hook
in same ch as previous sc and rep from *
to * across, ending with sc in tch.
ALL REMAINING ROWS: Rep Row Two.
NOTE: Tch = turning chain. Sc3tog is a
cluster stitch made up of three sc in the
last yo.

April

"We can, stitch by stitch, inch the world in a more positive direction. We do this by knitting for peace."
—BETTY CHRISTIANSEN

COLOR: Silver—Feminine Energy, Intuition, Flexibility

GEMSTONES: Diamond—Strength
Quartz Crystal—Insight

FLOWER: Daisy—Cheerfulness

TEA: Oolong

MUSIC TO STITCH BY: Gymnopédie No. 1 by Erik Satie

SCENT: Bergamot

SYMBOLS: Diamond, Star

THOUGHTS TO JOURNAL

Take some time to center
yourself, breathing in peace,
breathing out stress. With
each stitch you cast on or chain,
think to yourself . . . "peace."
Imagine this peace emanating
from the work in your hands
and flowing along the yarn
into the garment and out into
the world.

April

KNIT STITCH OF THE MONTH:
Honeycomb Slip-Stitch

Cast on an odd number of st.
ROW ONE (RS): Working in the front of the st.
knit.
ROW TWO (WS): K1, *sl 1, k1; rep from *.
ROW THREE: Working in the front of the st.,
knit.
ROW FOUR: K2, *sl 1, k1; rep from *,
end k1.

May

"Blessed are you, Spring, miracle child of the four seasons. With your wand of many colors you work magic in the corners of our darkness."

—JOYCE RUPP & MACRINA WIEDERKEHR

COLOR: Spring Green—Fertility, Renewal, Abundance

GEMSTONES: Emerald—Wisdom
Chrysoprase—Inner Peace

FLOWER: Lily of the Valley—Sweetness

TEA: Green

MUSIC TO STITCH BY: "To a Wild Rose" by Edward MacDowell

SCENT: Gardenia

SYMBOL: Flowers

THOUGHTS TO JOURNAL

If your knitting needle or
crochet hook were a magic wand,
what would you imbue into the
shawl you are creating? What
do the colors say? Imagine
the light of healing and peace
illuminating the stitches. Pray
the newness and hope of spring
into every stitch!

May

CROCHET STITCH OF THE MONTH:
Moss Stitch

Chain an odd number of sts.
FOUNDATION ROW: Sc in 3rd ch from hook.
ch 1, sk next ch, sc in next ch.
Rep from * to * across. Ch 2 (counts as tch
and 1st ch 1). Turn.
PATTERN ROW: Sk 1st sc, *sc in ch-1 space,
ch 1, sk next sc*. Rep from * to * across. End
with sc in ch 2 of previous row. Ch 2. Turn.
ALL REMAINING ROWS: Rep pattern for desired
length and width.

June

"There is no true solitude, except interior solitude."—THOMAS MERTON

COLOR: Yellow—Wisdom, Learning, Optimism

GEMSTONES: Pearl—Serenity
Moonstone—Calming

FLOWER: Rose—Friendship and Love

TEA: Rose Hip

MUSIC TO STITCH BY: Piano Sonata No. 14 in C-Sharp Minor from Op. 27:2 (Moonlight Sonata) by Ludwig van Beethoven

SCENT: Rose

SYMBOLS: Sun, Rose

THOUGHTS TO JOURNAL

Find a space that is quiet and
free of noise, and listen
carefully . . . what sounds can
you hear? Pay attention to your
breathing and heartbeat. Is
there a pattern you can develop
in everyday life that will
connect you with peace and
interior solitude?

CROCHET STITCH OF THE MONTH:
Portuguese-Inspired Stitch

Chain an odd number of sts + 1.

ROW ONE: Sc in 2nd ch from hook and in each ch across. Ch 4, turn.

ROW TWO: Sk 2 sc, dc in next sc, *ch 1, sk 1 sc, dc in next sc. Rep from * across. Ch 1, turn.

ROW THREE: Sc in 1st dc, *ch 1, sk ch-1 sp, sc in next dc. Rep from * across, placing last dc in 3rd ch of tch. Ch 4, turn.

ROW FOUR: Sk ch-1 sp, dc in next sc, * ch 1, sk ch-1 sp, dc in next sc. Rep from * across. Ch 1, turn.

NEXT ROW: Rep Rows 3 and 4 for pattern, until work measures desired length, ending with Row 4.

LAST ROW: Sc in each dc and ch-1 sp across. End off (87 sc). Ch-4 counts as 1 dc + ch-1 throughout. Weave in ends.

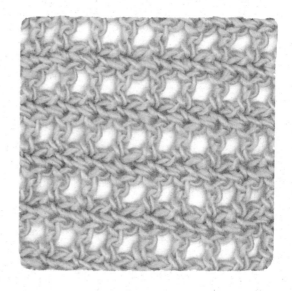

July

COLOR: Bright Red—Love, Energy, Warmth

GEMSTONES: Ruby—Happiness
Carnelian—Uplifting

FLOWER: Larkspur—Open Heart

TEA: Iced with Mint

MUSIC TO STITCH BY: "Clair de Lune"
by Claude Debussy

SCENT: Neroli

SYMBOL: Shell (look for one with a hole in it
so you can attach it to the fringe of a shawl)

THOUGHTS TO JOURNAL

Warm seasons surround us with
so much color—red geraniums,
yellow sunflower, orange daylilies,
green leaves, pink impatiens, blue
hydrangea, purple heliotrope. Take
a moment to rejoice with every color
you see and write a prayer of joy
and thanksgiving for these rainbow
blessings. What's your favorite?

July

KNIT STITCH OF THE MONTH:
Little Shell

Cast on a multiple of 7 + 2.
ROW ONE (RS): Knit.
ROW TWO: Purl.
ROW THREE: K2, *yo, p1, p3tog, p1, yo, k2;
rep from *.
ROW FOUR: Purl.

August

"The humble knitter sits in the center between heaven and earth. As she spins the yarn to make her sacred cloth, invisible threads connect her to both God and Mother Earth."
—SUSAN GORDON LYDON

COLORS: Wheat, Tan, Brown—Down-to-Earth, Stability

GEMSTONES: Peridot—Self-Esteem Sardonyx—Abundance

FLOWER: Gladiolus—Strength

TEA: Darjeeling

MUSIC TO STITCH BY: "Simple Gifts," traditional Shaker hymn arranged by Aaron Copland

SCENT: Vetiver

SYMBOL: Wheat Shaft

THOUGHTS TO JOURNAL

Place a piece of yarn in your journal or perhaps begin a prayer shawl "scrapbook" of your projects. Include cards, notes, and photos from your recipients. Use this as a source of reflection and meditation.

August

KNIT STITCH OF THE MONTH:
Sheaves of Wheat Stitch

Cast on a multiple of 6 + 1.
ROW ONE: *K4, p2, rep from * to last st, k1.
ROW TWO: P1, *k2, p4*.
ROW THREE: *Make wrap, p2, rep from * to last st, k1.
ROW 4: P1, *k2, p4*.
ROW 5: Knit all sts.
ROW 6: Purl all sts.
ROW 7: K1, *p2, k4*.
ROW 8: *P4, k2, rep from * to last st, p1.
ROW 9: K1, *p2, make wrap*.
ROW 10: *P4, k2, rep from * to last st, p1.

ROW 11: Knit all sts.
ROW 12: Purl all sts.
Rep these 12 rows for pattern.

NOTE: Make the wrap by placing the yarn in the back of your knitting; insert the right needle between the 4th and 5th stitches on left needle. Pull the yarn through, in between the stitches. Knit 4 stitches; next, use the left needle to pick up the loop on right needle and pass it over the 4 knit stitches. You may need to practice a few times to get the right tension.

September

"Everywhere, your web of life gives witness
to imagination, echoing our whispered word
proclaiming that all are one."
—MIRIAM THERESE WINTER

COLOR: Blue—Peace, Tranquility, Honesty

GEMSTONES: Sapphire—Fulfillment
Lapis Lazuli—Expression

FLOWER: Aster—Love

TEA: Lemon

MUSIC TO STITCH BY: Canon in D
by Johann Pachelbel

SCENT: Almond

SYMBOL: Autumn Leaf, Forget-Me-Not

THOUGHTS TO JOURNAL

As you knit or crochet, imagine that the skein of yarn from which you're working is connected to all the other shawl makers' yarns. Consider what this inter-connectedness means to you. How would you feel if the yarn you were working from was attached to a shawl maker with a different faith tradition or belief system? What would you weave into the shawl because of it?

September

KNIT STITCH OF THE MONTH:
Condo Stitch

Use any weight yarn and two sizes of needles. The smallest needle should be the suggested needle size for the yarn. The second needle should be a much larger size. Experiment for different results. The sample pictured is made with worsted weight yarn and sizes 9 US (5.5 mm) and 35 US (19 mm) needles. As you knit, pull down gently on stitches to even them out.

Knit one row. With larger needle, knit one row. Continue to knit every row, alternating needle sizes.

October

"Listen! The wind is rising, and the air is wild with leaves, we have had our summer evenings, now for October eves!"
—HUMBERT WOLFE

COLOR: Black—Wisdom, Strength, Self-Confidence

GEMSTONES: Opal—Spiritual Awareness
Tourmaline—Harmony

FLOWER: Marigold—Abundance

TEA: Black

MUSIC TO STITCH BY: Gnossiennes No. 1 by Erik Satie

SCENT: Rosemary

SYMBOLS: Pumpkin, Jack-o-Lantern

THOUGHTS TO JOURNAL

Autumn is here. The time of
year linked with earthy colors
of gold, brown, orange, red,
and green. Take some time this
season to bring your journal
outside and capture the moment.
As you sit and reflect, write
down your thoughts about the
autumnal season. Who knows,
perhaps a stray leaf will find its
way into your journal!

October

CROCHET STITCH OF THE MONTH:
Octagon Web Motif

Ch 8, sl st in first ch to form a ring.
ROUND ONE: Ch 4, [3 dc in ring, ch 1].
Rep 7 times, 2 dc in ring, sl st in 3rd ch.
ROUND TWO: Sl st in 1st sp, ch 4, 3 dc in same
sp, ch 1, [3 dc, ch 1] twice in each of next 7 sp,
2 dc in 1st sp, sl st in 3rd ch.
ROUND THREE: Sl st in 1st sp, ch 4, 3 dc in same
sp, *ch 1, 1 dc in next sp ch 1 [3 dc, ch 1, 3 dc]
in following sp, rep from * 6 more times,
ch 1, 1 dc in last sp, 1 ch, 2 dc in 1st sp, sl st
in 3rd ch.

ROUND FOUR: Sl st in 1st sp, ch 4, 3 dc in same
sp, * [ch 1, 1 dc in next sp] twice, ch 1, [3 dc,
ch 1, 3 dc] in following sp, rep from * 6 more
times, [ch 1, 1 dc in next sp] twice, ch 1, 2 dc
in 1st sp, sl st in 3rd ch.
ROUND FIVE: Sl st in 1st sp, ch 4, 3 dc in same
sp * [ch 1, 1 dc in next sp} 3 times, ch 1,
[3 dc, ch 1, 3 dc] in following sp, rep from
* 6 more times, [ch 1, 1 dc in next sp] 3 times,
ch 1, 2 dc in 1st sp, sl st in 3rd ch.
ALL REMAINING ROUNDS: Continue growing
the pattern by following the increases in dc
throughout motif—work to desired size,
fasten off.

November

"Hem your blessings with thankfulness so they don't unravel."
—ANONYMOUS

COLOR: Orange—Thoughtfulness, Vitality, Creativity

GEMSTONES: Yellow Topaz—Loyalty
Citrine—Clarity

FLOWER: Chrysanthemum—Optimism

TEA: Cinnamon or any spiced blend

MUSIC TO STITCH BY: "L'autunno" (also known as the "Danza Pastorale") from *The Four Seasons Suite* by Antonio Lucio Vivaldi

SCENT: Sandalwood

SYMBOL: Cornucopia

THOUGHTS TO JOURNAL

Knitters and crocheters know about unraveling! In this time of Thanksgiving when we count our blessings, consider how to handle the "unraveling" events of life. Can you hem them in with blessings? The next time your yarn tangles or unravels, consider meditating on life's blessings as you work through the knot. The recipient will be doubly blessed . . . and so will you!

November

CROCHET STITCH OF THE MONTH:
Cross Stitch

Chain a multiple of 2 to desired width.
ROW ONE: Turn. Ch1, *sk 1st st, dc in next;
working around dc just made, sc in the
skipped st.*
Rep from * to * across.
Rep Row One until desired length.

December

"The past is history. The future is a mystery and this moment is a gift. That is why this moment is called "the present."
—ANONYMOUS

COLOR: Green—Growth, Healing, Prosperity

GEMSTONES: Zircon—Understanding
Tanzanite—Contentment

FLOWER: Christmas Rose—Faith

TEA: Peppermint

MUSIC TO STITCH BY: "Silent Night" ("Stille Nach") by Franz Xaver Gruber

SCENT: Eucalyptus

SYMBOLS: Tree, Angel, Star

THOUGHTS TO JOURNAL

In this season of gift giving, stop, take a breath, and be present to this moment. Instead of worrying about all that you must do, remember that the present moment is, indeed, a gift. Pick up your knitting needles or crochet hook and enjoy some peace and quiet, then record your peace-filled thoughts in your journal. May you be wrapped in a shawl of peace this holiday season and the whole year through!

December

KNIT STITCH OF THE MONTH:
Berry Stitch

Cast on a multiple of 4 + 2.
ROW ONE (RS): Purl.
ROW TWO: K1, *(knit, purl, knit) into next st, p3tog, *rep to end, k1.
ROW THREE: Purl.
ROW FOUR: K1, *p3tog, (knit, purl, knit) into next st, * rep to end, k1.

The Patterns

VICKY GALO &
ROSANN GUZAUCKAS
Wethersfield,
Connecticut

Beginner's Shawl

WE SUGGEST THIS PATTERN FOR FIRST-TIME KNITTERS—it's made with knit stitches only, known as the Garter Stitch (p. 10). The same effect can be achieved with all purl stitches (p. 11), too—a fun way to master the purl stitch if it's new to you. Once you are comfortable with either stitch, you're ready to begin making a prayer shawl. Also, several shawl makers have told us they made their first shawl for someone who has or had cancer. The shawl pictured here was made in pink—the symbolic color of breast cancer survivors.

Skill Level
Easy

Finished Measurements
76 in. long and 19 in. wide

Yarn
- Approx 850 yd. lightweight bouclé yarn
- Shawl shown in Jo-Ann™ Sensations™ Rainbow Bouclé (88% acrylic/13% nylon; 853 yd./11 oz.), 1 skein Light Pink

Needles
- Size 10½ straight or circular needles (or size needed to obtain gauge)

Gauge
- 16 sts and 22 rows = 4 in. worked in Garter Stitch

NOTE: This Shawl can easily be made any size and with any yarn. When choosing yarn, refer to "Standard Yarn Weights," on p. 24. This will give you an indication of how much yarn you will need as well as what size needle. We recommend using large needles (size 10½ to size 15) and thick yarns for this type of shawl. You can use medium-weight yarns with large needles, too—the shawl will appear lacy. We do not recommend using small needles with thick yarn.

DIRECTIONS
CO 68 sts. Knit every row until shawl measures 76 in., or desired length. BO.

From
KRISTIN
SPURKLAND
Portland,
Oregon

Simple Shawl

"IN THINKING ABOUT MY GOALS IN DESIGNING THIS shawl," says Kristin Spurkland, "I decided that I wanted a simple, easy-to-memorize pattern, in a soft and soothing color. I wanted the process of knitting the shawl to be a reprieve from the excess busyness many of us experience in our daily lives."

Once the set-up rows are completed, the shawl consists of a two-row pattern repeat and is finished with a simple knit one, purl one bind-off. Thus the size can easily be adjusted—simply continue knitting the two-row pattern until the shawl is the desired size. Note, however, that the row gauge is very compressed, with almost three times as many rows per inch as stitches per inch. Therefore, the shawl becomes wider much faster than it becomes deeper.

Skill Level
Easy

Finished Measurements
• 60 in. long and 22½ in. deep,
  after blocking

Yarn
• Approx 510 yd. worsted weight yarn
Shawl shown in Louet™ Gems Worsted
(100% merino wool; 170 yd./3.5 oz.),
3 skeins #36 Linen Grey

Needles
• Size 8 circular needle, 24 in. long or longer
  (or size needed to obtain gauge)

Notions
• Tapestry needle

Gauge
• 13 sts and 35 rows = 4 in. worked
  in pattern, blocked

NOTE: The gauge will loosen up considerably when blocked.

Special Stitch

K1-RB: knit stitch in row below.

"'Tis the gift to be simple,
'tis the gift to be free,
'Tis the gift to come down where
we ought to be."

—FROM "SIMPLE GIFTS," TRADITIONAL SHAKER SONG, ELDER JOSEPH BRACKETT, 1848.'

DIRECTIONS

CO 3 sts.

SET-UP ROWS

ROW 1: (K1, m1) twice, k1. (5 sts).

ROWS 2 AND 4: Knit.

ROW 3: K1, m1, k1, k1-rb, k1, m1, k1. (7 sts).

BEGIN MAIN PATTERN

ROW 1 (RS): K1, m1, k1, (k1-rb, k1) to last 3 sts, k1-rb, k1, m1, k1.

ROW 2 (AND ALL WS ROWS): Knit. Rep these 2 rows until you have approximately 195 sts, ending with a RS row completed.

NEXT ROW (WS): BO in k1, p1 rib.

Weave in ends. Block shawl.

From
JANICE SHULZ
Heath, Ohio

Pocket Prayers

Pocket Shawl

"POCKET" PRAYER SHAWLS—SMALL RECTANGLES with a tassel at one end—can be carried in pockets or used in situations in which a large shawl is not appropriate or allowed, such as intensive care units of hospitals. Janice Schulz, founder of the Prayer Shawl Ministry at Christ Evangelical Lutheran Church in Heath, Ohio, designed these tiny shawls. In her shawl ministry, a pocket shawl is included whenever a prayer shawl is presented to someone, and one is often given to each member of a family dealing with a major illness or death. The pattern is simple and is a wonderful use of the left-over yarn from making a large shawl.

Skill Level
Easy

Finished Measurements
Approx 4 in. square

Yarn
• Approx 25 yd. worsted weight yarn

Needles
• Size 9 straight needles (or size needed to obtain gauge)

Gauge
• 16 sts and 28 rows = 4 in. worked in Garter Stitch

DIRECTIONS
CO 16 sts. Knit every row (Garter Stitch) until piece measures 4 in. BO all sts.

Add tassel (see p. 138) at the center of one end.

From
TISH HOAR
Mount Vernon,
Ohio

Prayer Cloth

PRAYER CLOTHS, ACCORDING TO TISH HOAR of Mount Vernon, Ohio, can be used to comfort the sick or to mark special occasions. Smaller prayer cloths can be tucked into purses and even helmets. For more information, go to http://sendingtroops prayers.bravehost.com.

Skill Level

Easy

Finished Meas   nents

Approx 12 in. squa

Yarn

• Approx 50 yd. worsted weight yarn

Needles

• Size 8 straight needles (or size needed to obtain desired gauge)

Gauge

• 16 sts and 34 rows = 4 in. worked in Garter Stitch

NOTE: Gauge is not crucial.

DIRECTIONS

CO on 4 sts.

ROW 1: Knit.

ROW 2: K2, inc 1 st in next st, k1.

ROW 3: K2, inc 1 st in next st, knit to end of row.

Rep Row 3 until square measures 12 in. along one side.

NEXT ROW: K1, k2tog, knit to end of row.

Rep this row until 5 sts remain.

NEXT ROW: K2, k2tog, k1.

BO remaining 4 sts.

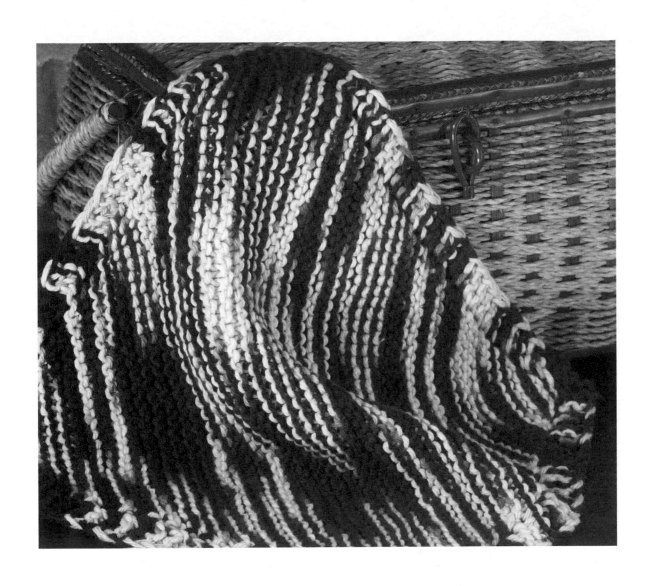

"The blessings flow from the person making the shawl, to the person receiving it, to the people who hear the stories, and on and on."

—JANIE RUPRIGHT

From
VICKY GALO
Berlin,
Connecticut

Recycled Sweater Shawl

THE TEXTURED RIBBON YARN was the inspiration for taking a favorite, outgrown hand-knit sweater and turning it into a shawl. I simply unraveled the sweater, washed and rewound the yarn, and began knitting.

If you decide to try this, choose a hand-knit sweater (most machine knits won't work) that is in very good condition to ensure that the yarn will withstand being reknit. You'll have to experiment with swatching and rely on your own interpretation to re-create this shawl, but it's a wonderful way to turn something old into something new.

Skill Level
Easy

Finished Measurements
• 72 in. long and 17 in. wide

Yarn
• Approx 1,100 yd. worsted weight yarn (less if shorter shawl is desired)
• Shawl shown in recycled light worsted weight ribbon yarn

Needles
• Size 10½ straight or circular needle (or size needed to obtain gauge)

Gauge
• 20 sts and 22 rows = 4 in. worked in pattern (gauge will vary depending on yarn used)

DIRECTIONS
CO 87 sts (multiple of 7 plus 3).

ROW 1: *K1, p1, k1, p4, rep from *; end k1, p1, k1.

ROW 2: *P1, k1, p1, k4, rep from *; end p1, k1, p1.

Work in pattern until shawl reaches 72 in. or desired length. BO loosely.

Caregiver's Prayer Shawl

From
JANET SEVERI
BRISTOW
Farmington,
Connecticut

SO MANY PEOPLE FIND THEMSELVES AS A CAREGIVER for someone who depends solely on them for all they need—physically, emotionally, and spiritually. They may be happy to be able to give something to those who are so dependent, but sometimes they can feel overwhelmed with the responsibility. This lacy shawl is meant to be light and airy, so as not to feel burdensome, but warm enough to offer comfort and soothe the sometimes-weary caregiver's soul. May it bless the wearer with serenity and peace.

Skill Level
Intermediate

Finished Measurements
• 61 in. long and 19 in. wide

Yarn
• Approx 840 yd. worsted weight yarn
• Shawl shown in Plymouth Yarn® Galway (100% wool, 210 yd./3.5 oz.), 4 skeins #756 Sunflower

Needles
• Size 11 straight or circular needle (or size needed to obtain gauge)

Notions
• Heart charms as desired

Gauge
• 12 sts and 13 rows = 4 in. worked in pattern

DIRECTIONS
CO 65 sts.

ROW 1: Knit.

ROW 2: Purl.

ROW 3: K2, *yo, p1, p3tog, p1, yo, k2, rep from * across.

ROW 4: Purl.

Rep these 4 rows until shawl measures 61 in. or desired length.

Block. Add fringe and add charms, if desired (see pp. 138–140).

From
VICKY GALO
Berlin,
Connecticut

Persephone Shawl

INSPIRED BY THE STORY OF PERSEPHONE AND Demeter from Greek mythology, this shawl is knitted in a knit one, purl one pattern, also known as Seed Stitch (p. 11). As the myth goes, Persephone (daughter of Demeter, the goddess of the harvest) was abducted to the Underworld by its lord, Hades. Demeter was able to get her back, but not before Persephone ate several pomegranate seeds, forcing her to return to the Underworld for a period of time each year. During this time, Demeter allows nothing to grow—hence the origin of our seasons.

The red color of this shawl, chosen to represent pomegranate seeds, also reminds us of the strong, feminine connection between mother and daughter. All knit stitches are knit into the back of the purl stitch below it, giving this shawl a distinctive seed look.

Skill Level
Easy

Finished Measurements
• 65 in. long and 17 in. wide

Yarn
• Approx 480 yd. chunky yarn
• Shawl shown in Caron® Simply Soft® Chunky (100% acrylic; 160 yd./5 oz.), 3 skeins #0007 Wine Country

Needles
• Size 11 straight or circular needle (or size needed to obtain gauge)

Gauge
• 11 sts and 15 rows = 4 in. worked in Seed Stitch

DIRECTIONS
CO 57 sts.

ROW 1: *K1-b, p1, rep from *; end k1.

ALL REMAINING ROWS: Sl 1; *p1, k1-b, rep from * to end.

BO and add tassels (see p. 138).

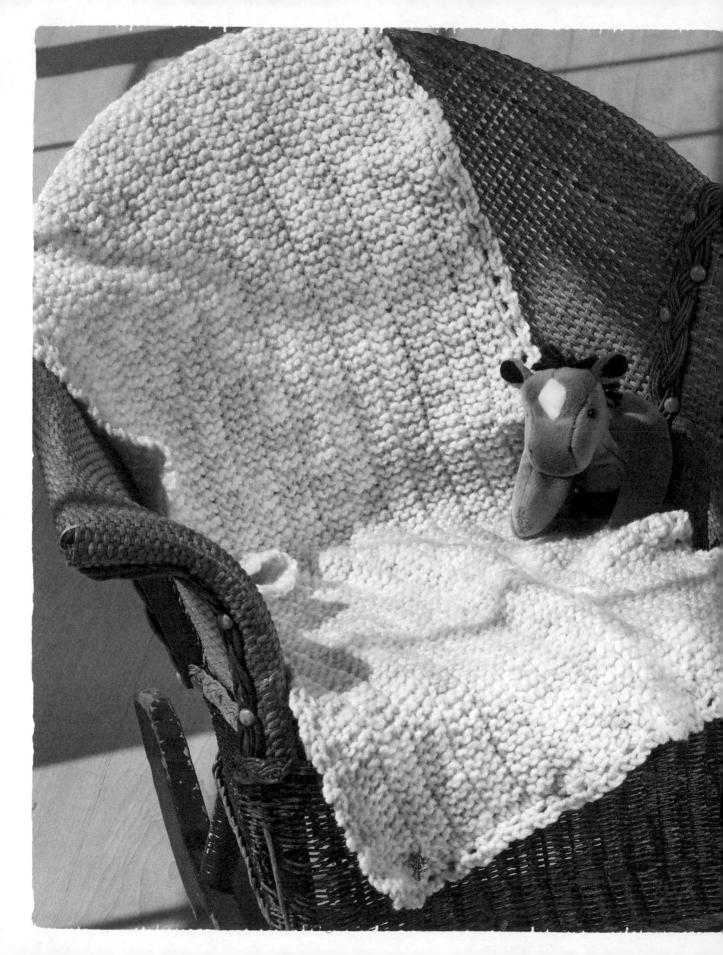

Baptism Shawls

THESE TWO SHAWLS ARE SMALLER VERSIONS OF THE ORIGINAL prayer shawl pattern, based on the knit three, purl three pattern. They can be used as baby gifts or knitted for baptisms, christenings, or baby naming ceremonies. They may also be given to any child as a source of comfort and solace. The first pattern is by Janet Severi Bristow and the second is from Susan Meader Tobias.

Skill Level
Easy

Finished Measurements
31 in. long and 13 in. wide (without edging)

Yarn
- Approx 350 yd. worsted weight yarn
- Shawl shown in Caron Perfect Match® (100% acrylic; 355 yd./7 oz.), 1 skein #7401 Baby Rainbow Ombre

Needles
- Size 10 straight or circular needles (or size needed to obtain gauge)
- Size G crochet hook (optional)

Gauge
- 15 sts and 25 rows = 4 in. worked in k3, p3 pattern

DIRECTIONS
CO 21 or 24 sts, or number for desired width (number of sts must be a multiple of 3).

ROW 1: K3, p3 across.

ROW 2: Knit the purl sts and purl the knit sts as they face you.

Work as established until shawl is 31 in. or desired length. BO all sts.

FINISHING
Add fringe (see p. 138) or crochet a simple ch-st edging, as follows: Attach yarn in one corner of shawl with a sc, *ch 5, sk 1 st, work 1 sc in next st, rep from * around shawl.

From
SUSAN MEADER
TOBIAS
Washington, D.C.

Triangle Baptism Shawl

Skill Level
Easy

Finished Measurements
45 in. long and 20 in. deep

Yarn
- Approx 180 yd. worsted weight yarn
- Shawl shown in Caron Perfect Match® (100% acrylic; 355 yd./7 oz.), 1 skein #7401 Baby Rainbow Ombre

Needles
- Size 13 straight or circular needle (or size needed to obtain gauge)

Notions
- Stitch markers

Gauge
- 12 sts and 14 rows = 4 in. worked in 3-St Pattern

DIRECTIONS
CO 3 sts.

ROW 1: Inc 1 st in each st. (6 sts)

ROW 2: K3, p3 across.

ROWS 3–99: Inc 1 st at beginning of every row, maintaining the 3-St Pattern by purling the knits and knitting the purls as they face you. You may need to use markers to help keep track of the 3-st rep, because each row will be different.

BO loosely.

From
RITA GLOD
Enfield,
Connecticut

Original Crocheted Prayer Shawl

RITA GLOD DEVELOPED THIS CROCHETED SHAWL pattern to follow its knitted sister pattern and brought it to her local Prayer Shawl Ministry in Connecticut. Like the knit and purl stitches, single crochets and double crochets combine in the symbolism of threes.

Skill Level
Easy

Finished Measurements
18 in. x 70 in., excluding fringe

Yarn
• Approximately 1,000 yd. DK weight yarn
• Shawl shown in yarn from Independence Farm of Thomaston, Connecticut (100% alpaca; 250 yd./4 oz.), 4 skeins Bay Black

Hook
• Size J/10/6 mm (or size needed to obtain gauge)

Optional Materials
Stone chip beads and clear nylon or elastic beading filament to embellish tassels as shown in photo on p. 104

Gauge
• 11 sts and 5 dc rows = 4 in. in pattern st

NOTE: Ch-3 counts as 1 dc throughout.

DIRECTIONS
Ch 63 (or desired width) loosely.

ROW 1: Sc in 2nd ch from hook and in each ch across. Ch 3, turn. (62 sc).

ROW 2: Sk 1st sc, dc in each sc across. Ch 3, turn. (62 dc counting t-ch).

ROW 3: Sk 1st dc, dc in each dc across. Ch 3, turn.

ROW 4: Rep Row 3. Ch 1, turn.

ROW 5: Sc in each dc across. Ch 3, turn.

Rep Rows 2–5 for pattern until work measures 70 in. or desired length, ending with a Row 5. End off.

"May you feel the love in each stitch of this shawl. May it warm your heart and keep you from harm. This is my prayer for you."

—LALENYA LOPEZ

TASSEL FRINGE

Cut 144 22-in. lengths of yarn. Fold each strand in half, then attach 8 strands of fringe in a group, 9 groups evenly spaced along each short side. Tie in an overhand knot close to the shawl, adding a strand of beads if desired.

To add the beads, knot one end of a 10-in. (or longer) segment of plastic filament (thread will tear through the soft yarn fibers) and secure the knot with a dab of glue. Let the glue dry, then thread seven or more little beads on the strand, and knot to secure. Thread the remaining length of filament through a needle and stitch the bead strand into the top of the tassel. Secure with a knot, and snip off any excess filament.

From
VICKY GALO
Berlin,
Connecticut

Milk Fiber Shawl

READ THE LABEL OF THIS YARN CAREFULLY. "MILK fiber." We've heard of hay being spun into gold, and bamboo, soy, and corn being transformed into decadent textural fibers, but who would have ever thought of milk? May this shawl be a reminder for you to nurture your soul.

Skill Level

Easy

Finished Measurements

17 in. x 78 in., excluding fringe

Yarn

- Approximately 624 yd. worsted weight yarn
- Shawl shown in Rosarios4® Cappuccino Cream (70% Australian wool/30% milk fiber; 104 yd./1.75 oz.), 6 skeins #49

Hook

- Size I/9/5.50 mm (or size needed to obtain gauge)

Gauge

- 3 loops and 4 rows = 4 in. in pattern st. Gauge is not critical in this pattern.

Special Stitches

- Knots = Rigmarole or Lover's Knot stitch: *Extend loop on hook until it is 1 in. long or desired length, ch 1 while grasping base of st so working yarn can't pull on loop and length is maintained, sc in back/single loop only of extended ch. Rep from * until desired number of knot sts is made.

DIRECTIONS

ROW 1: Ch 2, sc in 2nd ch from hook, work 36 knots. Turn.

ROW 2: Sc in 5th sc from hook, *work 2 knots, sk 1 sc, sc in next sc. Rep from * to end. Turn. (17 loops).

ROW 3: *Work 2 knots, sk 1 sc, sc in next sc. Rep from * to end. Turn. (17 loops).

Rep Row 3 for pattern until shawl measures 78 in. or desired length. End off. Weave in ends.

FRINGE

Cut 68 12-in. lengths of yarn. Fold each strand in half, then attach 2 strands of fringe in each loop. Tie groups of 2 in an overhand knot close to the shawl, then add another row of knots.

Granny Square—Edged Shawl

THIS SHAWL INCORPORATES A VARIATION ON the granny square along the edges. It's a great way to experiment with a motif other than the classic granny square. The shawl is shown in worsted weight yarn. Sport weight can be used for a lighter shawl.

Skill Level
Easy

Finished Measurements
24 in. x 70 in.

Yarn
- Approximately 1,890 yd. worsted weight yarn in three colors (945 yd. color A, 630 yd. color B, and 315 yd. color C)
- Shawl shown in Caron Simply Soft (100% acrylic; 315 yd./6 oz.), 3 skeins #9738 Violet (color A), and Lion Brand® Vanna's Choice® (100% acrylic; 170 yd./3.5 oz.), 2 skeins #134 Terra Cotta (color B), and 1 skein #170 Pea Green (color C)

Hooks
- Size D/3/3.25 mm and F/5/3.75 mm (or sizes needed to obtain gauge)

Optional Materials
- 16 beads or decorative shank buttons

Gauge
- 11 sts and 6 rows = 4 in. in pattern st for Body

NOTES:
- Ch-3 counts as 1 dc throughout.
- In Motif, ch-5 counts as 1 dc + 2 ch.

DIRECTIONS

MOTIF
MAKE 8 in this color order, 4 reversing colors A and B:

With size D hook and color A, ch 4, sl st in 1st ch to form ring.

RND 1: Ch 3, 15 dc in ring, join with sl st in top of beg ch. (16 dc, ch-3 counts as 1 dc here and throughout).

RND 2: Sl st between beg ch-3 and next dc of prev rnd, ch 5 (counts as 1 dc + ch 2), [dc in between next 2 dc, ch 2] 15 times, join rnd with sl st in 3rd ch of beg ch-5. (16 ch-2 sp)

RND 3: Sl st in next ch-2 sp, ch 3, 2 dc in same sp, [ch 1, sk next dc, 3 dc in next ch-2 sp] 15 times, ch 1, sk next dc, join rnd with sl st in top of beg ch. End off. (16 3-dc shells)

RND 4: Join color B in any ch-1 sp, sc in same sp, *[ch 3, sk next 3 dc, sc in next ch-1 sp] 3 times, ch 5 (corner loop made), sc in next ch-1 sp. Rep from * 3 times more, omitting final sc of last rep, join rnd with sl st in first sc 12 ch-3 loops + 4 ch-5 corner loops).

RND 5: Sl st in next ch-3 sp, ch 3, 2 dc in same sp, [ch 1, sk next sc, 3 dc in next ch-3 sp] twice, ch 1, [5 dc, ch 2, 5 dc] in next ch-5 sp, *[ch 1, sk next sc, 3 dc in next ch-3 sp] 3 times, ch 1, [5 dc, ch 2, 5 dc] in next ch-5 sp. Rep from * 2 times more, ch 1, sk next sc, join rnd with sl st in top of beg ch (76 dc/19 per side). End off.

RND 6: Join color C in any ch-2 corner sp, ch 3, [tr, dc] in same sp, *[dc between next 2 dc] 4 times; ** dc in next ch-1 sp, [dc in between next 2 dc] twice **; rep from ** to ** twice more; dc in next ch-1 sp, [dc in sp between next 2 dc] 4 times, [dc, tr, dc] in next corner ch-2 sp. Rep from * 3 times more, omitting final [dc, tr, dc] of last rep, join rnd with sl st in top of beg ch. (80 dc/20 per side + 4 tr) End off.

JOINING

Make 2 strips of 4 squares each, alternating color pattern.

With RS together, whip st squares together through front loops only using color C.

BODY

Hold 1 assembled strip with RS facing and long edge on top, join color C in first tr.

ROW 1 (RS): Ch 3, * dc in next 20 dc, dc in next seam, rep from * 3 times more; dc in last tr (85 dc). End off.

ROW 2 (RS): With RS facing, join color A in top of beg ch-3 of prev row, ch 4, tr in each dc to end. Ch 3, turn. (85 tr)

ROW 3 (WS): Sk 1st tr, dc in each tr to end. Ch 4, turn.

ROW 4: Sk 1st dc, tr in each dc to end. Ch 3, turn.

Rep Rows 3 & 4 for pattern until shawl is 64 in. or 6 in. less than desired length, ending with a Row 3. End off.

LAST ROW: With RS facing and color C, rep Row 1.

ATTACH SECOND STRIP

With RS facing each other, whip st 2nd strip to just-finished shawl body through front loops only using color C lining up sts as you go.

OPTIONAL EDGING

Hold shawl with RS facing and long side at top. With size F hook and color of choice, join yarn in first dc. *Sk next 2 dc, 5 dc in next dc, sk next 2 dc, sl st in next dc. Rep from * around shawl (counting end st of each row of center section as a dc), adjust sts slightly so that last sl st is made in joining sl st. End off.

FINISHING

Weave in all ends. Block if desired.

Affix beads or decorative buttons to the center hole of each motif. If using buttons, stitch 2 back to back so they can be viewed from either side.

Stitch Along

Projects I Want to Make

Pattern Name ....

Pattern Location ....
(magazine or book title & page, web address)

Yarn ....

Number of Balls/Skeins ....

Number of Yards/Meters per Ball/Skein ....

Gauge ....

Needles/Hooks ....

Notions ....

Notes ....

Pattern Name ....

Pattern Location ....
(magazine or book title & page, web address)

Yarn ....

Number of Balls/Skeins ....

Number of Yards/Meters per Ball/Skein ....

Gauge ....

Needles/Hooks ....

Notions ....

Notes ....

Pattern Name --

Pattern Location --
(magazine or book title & page, web address)

Yarn --

Number of Balls/Skeins --

Number of Yards/Meters per Ball/Skein --------------------------------------

Gauge ---

Needles/Hooks ---

Notions ---

Notes ---

Pattern Name --

Pattern Location --
(magazine or book title & page, web address)

Yarn --

Number of Balls/Skeins --

Number of Yards/Meters per Ball/Skein --------------------------------------

Gauge ---

Needles/Hooks ---

Notions ---

Notes ---

Projects I Want to Make

Pattern Name ....

Pattern Location ....
(magazine or book title & page, web address)

Yarn ....

Number of Balls/Skeins ....

Number of Yards/Meters per Ball/Skein ....

Gauge ....

Needles/Hooks ....

Notions ....

Notes ....

Pattern Name ....

Pattern Location ....
(magazine or book title & page, web address)

Yarn ....

Number of Balls/Skeins ....

Number of Yards/Meters per Ball/Skein ....

Gauge ....

Needles/Hooks ....

Notions ....

Notes ....

Pattern Name ....

Pattern Location ....
(magazine or book title & page, web address)

Yarn ....

Number of Balls/Skeins ....

Number of Yards/Meters per Ball/Skein ....

Gauge ....

Needles/Hooks ....

Notions ....

Notes ....

Pattern Name ....

Pattern Location ....
(magazine or book title & page, web address)

Yarn ....

Number of Balls/Skeins ....

Number of Yards/Meters per Ball/Skein ....

Gauge ....

Needles/Hooks ....

Notions ....

Notes ....

Projects I Want to Make

Pattern Name

Pattern Location
(magazine or book title & page, web address)

Yarn

Number of Balls/Skeins

Number of Yards/Meters per Ball/Skein

Gauge

Needles/Hooks

Notions

Notes

Pattern Name

Pattern Location
(magazine or book title & page, web address)

Yarn

Number of Balls/Skeins

Number of Yards/Meters per Ball/Skein

Gauge

Needles/Hooks

Notions

Notes

Pattern Name ···

Pattern Location ··
(magazine or book title & page, web address)

Yarn ···

Number of Balls/Skeins ··

Number of Yards/Meters per Ball/Skein ···

Gauge ···

Needles/Hooks ···

Notions ··

Notes ···

Pattern Name ···

Pattern Location ··
(magazine or book title & page, web address)

Yarn ···

Number of Balls/Skeins ··

Number of Yards/Meters per Ball/Skein ···

Gauge ···

Needles/Hooks ···

Notions ··

Notes ···

Projects I Want to Make

Pattern Name ....

Pattern Location ....
(magazine or book title & page, web address)

Yarn ....

Number of Balls/Skeins ....

Number of Yards/Meters per Ball/Skein ....

Gauge ....

Needles/Hooks ....

Notions ....

Notes ....

Pattern Name ....

Pattern Location ....
(magazine or book title & page, web address)

Yarn ....

Number of Balls/Skeins ....

Number of Yards/Meters per Ball/Skein ....

Gauge ....

Needles/Hooks ....

Notions ....

Notes ....

Pattern Name ....

Pattern Location ....
(magazine or book title & page, web address)

Yarn ....

Number of Balls/Skeins ....

Number of Yards/Meters per Ball/Skein ....

Gauge ....

Needles/Hooks ....

Notions ....

Notes ....

Pattern Name ....

Pattern Location ....
(magazine or book title & page, web address)

Yarn ....

Number of Balls/Skeins ....

Number of Yards/Meters per Ball/Skein ....

Gauge ....

Needles/Hooks ....

Notions ....

Notes ....

Projects I've Made

Pattern Name ....

Pattern Location ....
(magazine or book title & page, web address)

Yarn ....

Number of Balls/Skeins ....

Number of Yards/Meters per Ball/Skein ....

Gauge ....

Needles/Hooks ....

Notions ....

Notes ....

Pattern Name ....

Pattern Location ....
(magazine or book title & page, web address)

Yarn ....

Number of Balls/Skeins ....

Number of Yards/Meters per Ball/Skein ....

Gauge ....

Needles/Hooks ....

Notions ....

Notes ....

Pattern Name --

Pattern Location --
(magazine or book title & page, web address)

Yarn ---

Number of Balls/Skeins --

Number of Yards/Meters per Ball/Skein ---------------------------------------

Gauge --

Needles/Hooks --

Notions --

Notes --

Pattern Name --

Pattern Location --
(magazine or book title & page, web address)

Yarn ---

Number of Balls/Skeins --

Number of Yards/Meters per Ball/Skein ---------------------------------------

Gauge --

Needles/Hooks --

Notions --

Notes --

Projects I've Made

Pattern Name ....

Pattern Location ....
(magazine or book title & page, web address)

Yarn ....

Number of Balls/Skeins ....

Number of Yards/Meters per Ball/Skein ....

Gauge ....

Needles/Hooks ....

Notions ....

Notes ....

Pattern Name ....

Pattern Location ....
(magazine or book title & page, web address)

Yarn ....

Number of Balls/Skeins ....

Number of Yards/Meters per Ball/Skein ....

Gauge ....

Needles/Hooks ....

Notions ....

Notes ....

Pattern Name ....

Pattern Location ....
(magazine or book title & page, web address)

Yarn ....

Number of Balls/Skeins ....

Number of Yards/Meters per Ball/Skein ....

Gauge ....

Needles/Hooks ....

Notions ....

Notes ....

Pattern Name ....

Pattern Location ....
(magazine or book title & page, web address)

Yarn ....

Number of Balls/Skeins ....

Number of Yards/Meters per Ball/Skein ....

Gauge ....

Needles/Hooks ....

Notions ....

Notes ....

Projects I've Made

Pattern Name ....

Pattern Location ....
(magazine or book title & page, web address)

Yarn ....

Number of Balls/Skeins ....

Number of Yards/Meters per Ball/Skein ....

Gauge ....

Needles/Hooks ....

Notions ....

Notes ....

Pattern Name ....

Pattern Location ....
(magazine or book title & page, web address)

Yarn ....

Number of Balls/Skeins ....

Number of Yards/Meters per Ball/Skein ....

Gauge ....

Needles/Hooks ....

Notions ....

Notes ....

Pattern Name ....

Pattern Location ....
(magazine or book title & page, web address)

Yarn ....

Number of Balls/Skeins ....

Number of Yards/Meters per Ball/Skein ....

Gauge ....

Needles/Hooks ....

Notions ....

Notes ....

Pattern Name ....

Pattern Location ....
(magazine or book title & page, web address)

Yarn ....

Number of Balls/Skeins ....

Number of Yards/Meters per Ball/Skein ....

Gauge ....

Needles/Hooks ....

Notions ....

Notes ....

My Yarn Stash

Name and Brand ....

Color ....

Fiber Content ....

Weight ....

Number of Yards/Meters per Ball/Skein ....

Number of Balls/Skeins ....

Notes ....

....

Name and Brand ....

Color ....

Fiber Content ....

Weight ....

Number of Yards/Meters per Ball/Skein ....

Number of Balls/Skeins ....

Notes ....

....

Name and Brand ....

Color ....

Fiber Content ....

Weight ....

Number of Yards/Meters per Ball/Skein ....

Number of Balls/Skeins ....

Notes ....

....

Name and Brand ....

Color ....

Fiber Content ....

Weight ....

Number of Yards/Meters per Ball/Skein ....

Number of Balls/Skeins ....

Notes ....

....

My Yarn Stash

Name and Brand ....

Color ....

Fiber Content ....

Weight ....

Number of Yards/Meters per Ball/Skein ....

Number of Balls/Skeins ....

Notes ....

....

Name and Brand ....

Color ....

Fiber Content ....

Weight ....

Number of Yards/Meters per Ball/Skein ....

Number of Balls/Skeins ....

Notes ....

....

Name and Brand ....

Color ....

Fiber Content ....

Weight ....

Number of Yards/Meters per Ball/Skein ....

Number of Balls/Skeins ....

Notes ....

....

Name and Brand ....

Color ....

Fiber Content ....

Weight ....

Number of Yards/Meters per Ball/Skein ....

Number of Balls/Skeins ....

Notes ....

....

My Yarn Stash

Name and Brand ....

Color ....

Fiber Content ....

Weight ....

Number of Yards/Meters per Ball/Skein ....

Number of Balls/Skeins ....

Notes ....

....

Name and Brand ....

Color ....

Fiber Content ....

Weight ....

Number of Yards/Meters per Ball/Skein ....

Number of Balls/Skeins ....

Notes ....

....

Name and Brand --

Color --

Fiber Content --

Weight --

Number of Yards/Meters per Ball/Skein -----------------------------

Number of Balls/Skeins --

Notes --

Name and Brand --

Color --

Fiber Content --

Weight --

Number of Yards/Meters per Ball/Skein -----------------------------

Number of Balls/Skeins --

Notes --

My Yarn Stash

Name and Brand ....

Color ....

Fiber Content ....

Weight ....

Number of Yards/Meters per Ball/Skein ....

Number of Balls/Skeins ....

Notes ....

....

Name and Brand ....

Color ....

Fiber Content ....

Weight ....

Number of Yards/Meters per Ball/Skein ....

Number of Balls/Skeins ....

Notes ....

....

Knitting Needles

U.S.	1	2	3	4	5	6	7	8	9	10	10½	11	13	15	17	19	35	50
Metric	2.25	2.75	3.25	3.5	3.75	4	4.5	5	5.5	6	6.5	8	9	10	12.75	15	19	25
Straight 10″	☐	☐	☐	☐	☐	☐	☐	☐	☐	☐	☐	☐	☐	☐	☐	☐	☐	☐
Straight 14″	☐	☐	☐	☐	☐	☐	☐	☐	☐	☐	☐	☐	☐	☐	☐	☐	☐	☐
Double-Pointed	☐	☐	☐	☐	☐	☐	☐	☐	☐	☐	☐	☐	☐	☐	☐	☐	☐	☐
Circular 12″	☐	☐	☐	☐	☐	☐	☐	☐	☐	☐	☐	☐	☐	☐	☐	☐	☐	☐
Circular 16″	☐	☐	☐	☐	☐	☐	☐	☐	☐	☐	☐	☐	☐	☐	☐	☐	☐	☐
Circular 20″	☐	☐	☐	☐	☐	☐	☐	☐	☐	☐	☐	☐	☐	☐	☐	☐	☐	☐
Circular 24″	☐	☐	☐	☐	☐	☐	☐	☐	☐	☐	☐	☐	☐	☐	☐	☐	☐	☐
Circular 29″	☐	☐	☐	☐	☐	☐	☐	☐	☐	☐	☐	☐	☐	☐	☐	☐	☐	☐
Circular 32″	☐	☐	☐	☐	☐	☐	☐	☐	☐	☐	☐	☐	☐	☐	☐	☐	☐	☐
Circular 36″	☐	☐	☐	☐	☐	☐	☐	☐	☐	☐	☐	☐	☐	☐	☐	☐	☐	☐

Crochet Hooks

U.S.	B 1	C 2	D 3	E 4	F 5	G 6	H 8	I 9	J 10	K 10.5	L 11	M/N 13	N/P 15	P/Q	Q	S
Metric	2.25	2.75	3.25	3.5	3.75	4	5	5.5	6	6.5	8	9	10	15	16	19
	☐	☐	☐	☐	☐	☐	☐	☐	☐	☐	☐	☐	☐	☐	☐	☐

Fringes and Edges

When you finish a shawl, it is nice to add finishing touches such as fringe, tassels, macramé edging, or even a simple crocheted edge. Personalize the shawl for the recipient by adding pretty beads, ornaments, or charms that have special meaning. Embellishments not only add beauty, but can also be used as a source of meditation and reflection for the shawl recipient.

TASSEL

Cut a piece of cardboard to the length desired for the tassel. Wrap yarn around the cardboard (the more yarn, the thicker the tassel). When finished, thread a length of yarn on a needle and slide it under the top wraps of the tassel. Tie tightly, and do not trim (use the strands to attach the tassel to the project). Slide a scissors blade under the bottom wraps and cut. Tie a second length of yarn around the tassel about ½ in. from the top and tie tightly. Trim the ends as desired.

POMPOM

Cut two cardboard circles the diameter of the desired pompom. Cut a 1-in.-diameter hole out of the middle of both circles. Cut a small wedge out of both, then hold the circles together with these openings aligned. Wrap the yarn tightly all the way around both circles. When finished, slide a scissors blade between the two circles and cut the yarn around the outer edge. Wrap a length of yarn around the strands between the circles and tie tightly. Slip the circles off the completed pompom and trim the pompom evenly, leaving the tie intact to sew onto the project.

CHARMS

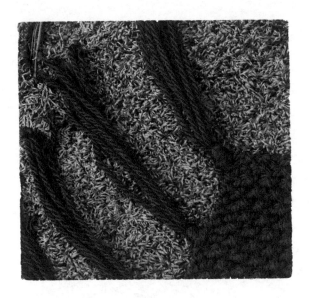

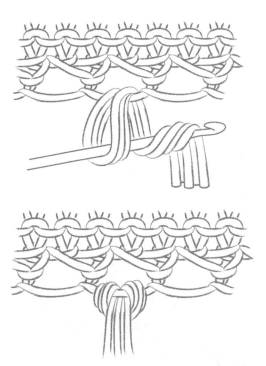

FRINGE

Cut yarn to the length specified in the pattern (or twice the length of desired fringe; i.e., 16-in. lengths for an 8-in. fringe). Holding together as many lengths as desired, fold lengths in half, insert crochet hook into the first stitch on either the cast-on or bound-off edge, pull up a loop by catching the length of fringe at its center point, and pull the loose ends through the loop. Pull to tighten. Repeat across edge. Trim fringe to make even, as needed.

BEADS

SHELLS

DOUBLE-KNOT FRINGE

Follow the directions for fringe. After completing the fringe as described on p. 139, turn the shawl so the right side of the work is facing you. Work knots as shown in the diagram at right.

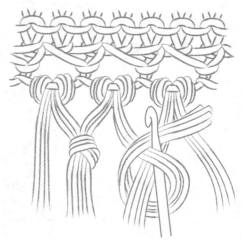

MACRAMÉ FRINGE

For an open, airy, macramé look, follow the
directions for the double-knot fringe on
the facing page, but repeat the row of knots as
often as desired. The fiber and weight of the
yarn will change this look from shawl to shawl:
Lightweight yarns create an airy web; bulkier
yarns weave a warm, substantial net.

Make a Sachet or Gift Bag

After you have added a pretty edge to your prayer shawl, it's delightful to add some scent to include with the presentation. In The Prayer Shawl Year Chapter (p. 27), we've suggested different essential oils for each month, which you can use for a sachet.

TO MAKE A SACHET

To make a sachet, simply cut out a small (5 in. by 5 in.) square of netting or lightweight fabric. (The easiest to use is netting that comes on wide rolls in the ribbon and/or bridal section of fabric and craft stores—it comes in a range of colors.) You'll also need two or three cotton balls, and a few inches of thin ribbon or pieces of yarn to tie the finished sachet.

Place a few drops of essential oil onto each cotton ball. If you have dried flowers you'd like to include, then all the better! Place the scented cotton balls in the center of a netting square, gather up the corners, and tie closed with a yarn or ribbon bow.

You may wish to let the shawl recipient decide whether or not they want their shawl scented. If so, place the sachet in a small plastic bag with a note explaining the sachet's use. Be aware that some people are allergic to or do not care for certain scents.

TO KNIT OR CROCHET A GIFT BAG

A beautiful project deserves a beautiful package. You can knit, crochet, or sew an easy gift bag for your shawl, and the fabric version is quick to make if you are pressed for time.

Fold the completed shawl into a square or desired shape. Measure the size of the folded shawl and knit or crochet a square of equal size. Knit or crochet a second square, but extend the length by 4 in. to 6 in. Sew three sides together, leaving the extended length at the top, creating a flap. Tie a folded piece of yarn or ribbon long enough to tie around the entire package into the center edge of the flap. Wrap the ribbon all the way around the bag and secure with a bow.

TO SEW A GIFT BAG

This project makes three bags. Cut 1 yd. of 45-in.-wide fabric, fold over a small hem on each raw end, and sew it down. Fold the fabric in half with right sides facing each other and hemmed edges touching. Keeping the fold at the bottom, cut into three even segments. Stitch the sides of each segment closed to make a bag. Turn right side out and place the shawl into the bag. Secure with yarn or ribbon. For larger, bulkier shawls, use wider fabric or make two bags out of 1 yd. of 45-in.-wide fabric.

Colors & Symbology

Colors, gems, and other symbols are noted in each month of The Prayer Shawl Year chapter. Here is a little more information on colors and symbols, so that you can customize designs of your own.

There are many lists of color meanings and symbology; ours is a blend from many different sources we've explored through the years. We invite you to use it as a starting point for inspiration. We naturally select colors to which we are attracted, but keep in mind that each of us has different emotional reactions to color. You may not be a "pink person," but someone else is. So try to be open to knitting with all colors. A hue that you don't particularly care for might thrill someone else!

Color Chart

RED: love, passion, respect, energy, enthusiasm, courage, vigor, health, understanding, motivation, strength, warmth

PINK: friendship, compassion, sensitivity, generosity, soothing, warm-heartedness, nurturing, admiration, gratitude, appreciation, admiration, sympathy

ORANGE: thoughtfulness, vitality, creativity, energy, warmth, vibrance, autumn, summer

YELLOW: wisdom, learning, optimism, intuition, faith, well-being, friendship, energy, happiness, sociability, joy, gladness, goodness

GREEN: earth, healing, prosperity, fertility, clarity, sympathy, hope, renewal, health, confidence, abundance, growth, life, permanence, peace, relaxation, spring

AQUA: courage, balance, harmony, stability

BLUE: water, healing, meditation, intuition, peace, tranquility, honesty, loyalty, communication, sincerity, wisdom, spirituality, eternity, self-esteem, universal color, coolness, calmness, unity

INDIGO: wisdom, insight, instinct, spiritual nature

VIOLET: spirit, spirituality, intuition, truth, memory, nostalgia, humility, comfort during grief or mourning, peace

PURPLE: power, leadership, royalty, truth, justice, temperance, spirituality, wisdom

BROWN: wholesomeness, honesty, steadfastness, simplicity, friendliness, dependability, practical, down-to-earth, warmth

BEIGE/TAN: optimism, simplicity, calmness

BLACK: self-confidence, strength, absorbs negativity, mature wisdom, harmony

WHITE: spirit, light, air, innocence, protection, peace, purity, gentleness, perfection, holiness, maidenhood, illumination, reverence, humility, winter

GOLD: masculine energy, enlightenment, sacred, durable

SILVER: feminine energy, flexibility

GRAY: strength, balance, wisdom

SYMBOLISM

Sewn onto a shawl or tied into the fringe, charms, beads, and gemstones add decoration and still more symbolic meaning into a shawl.

Symbolism

ANIMALS

Bird: spirituality, mental clarity, communication

Butterfly: transformation, beauty, spontaneity, freedom, resurrection

Bee: fertility, harmony, community, organization

Dragonfly: harmony, emotions, happiness, new perspectives, light

Lion: community, protection, strength, love, balance, harmony, peace, propriety

Fish: peace, prosperity, abundance

Dolphin: healing, intelligence, breath, creativity

Tiger: strength, power, motherly devotion

Turtle: longevity, fertility, moon, wisdom

Frog: fertility, inspiration

Dog: love, friendship, fidelity

Cat: wisdom, love, affection

Bear: strength, protection, relaxation, curiosity

SHAPES

Circle: marriage, beginning, eternity

Triangle: trinity, woman, creative intellect

Spiral: journey, feminine wisdom, transformation, introspection

Heart: love, unity, friendship

Square: balance, completion

RELIGIOUS SYMBOLS

Cross: Christianity, sacrifice, salvation, creation, redemption

Star of David: Judaism

Yin/Yang: balance, dualism

Wheel: universe, progress

Claddagh: loyalty, friendship, romantic love

Pentacle: Wiccan symbol of protection

Dreamcatcher: Ojibwa (Chippewa) symbol of protection; traps negative spirits

Gemstones

Garnet: faithfulness

Rose quartz: unconditional love

Amethyst: sincerity

Onyx: relaxation, strength

Aquamarine: calm, protection

Bloodstone: courage

Diamond: strength

Quartz crystal: insight

Emerald: wisdom

Chrysoprase: inner peace

Pearl: serenity

Moonstone: calming, intuition

Ruby: happiness

Carnelian: uplifting

Peridot: self-esteem

Sardonyx: abundance, courage

Sapphire: fulfillment

Lapis lazuli: expression

Opal: spiritual awareness

Tourmaline: harmony

Topaz: loyalty

Citrine: clarity

Zircon: understanding

Turquoise: contentment, protection

How to Start a Prayer Shawl Ministry

Forming a Prayer Shawl Ministry group is a great way to involve many people in meeting the needs of others, whether in a faith community, hospice, hospital, circle of friends, or knitting or crocheting group. We even know of a yoga group that incorporates shawl making into their practice. If you belong to a faith community, meet with clergy and staff to see if the ministry could be introduced there. If you will be bringing this to the community in which you live, find a space that could accommodate your needs, such as a library, community center, senior center, classroom for continuing adult education, and so on. Or you can also simply gather a friend or two and meet in each other's homes.

TO INVITE MEMBERS INTO YOUR PRAYER SHAWL MINISTRY GROUP, CONSIDER THE FOLLOWING:

- Place an ad in your church bulletin, your organization's newsletter, the local newspaper, or publications or brochures sent out by community centers, libraries, senior centers, and continuing adult education offices. Or make a flier or sign-up sheet and post it on bulletin boards at these locations.
- Strive to be as inclusive as possible in your search for group members—extending the invitation to knitters in faith communities different than your own opens the door for interfaith dialogue and better understanding of different beliefs and cultures.

- Visit www.shawlministry.com and use the downloadable brochure as a handout to give to those interested in joining your group. Or schedule a Prayer Shawl Ministry Workshop by contacting us at shawlministry@yahoo.com, attn: Janet. For further information, see the Workshop page on the Shawl Ministry website for details.

AT YOUR FIRST MEETING, YOU WILL WANT TO:
- Decide how often you will meet—weekly, bimonthly, or monthly—and finalize a time.
- Have a brainstorming session, discussing the style or format of your Prayer Shawl Ministry meetings and who the prayer shawl recipients will be.
- If you'll be supplying shawls to a shelter, hospital, or oncology center on a regular basis, inquire about the approximate number of shawls that will be required and whether your group can meet that goal.
- Decide on a method for recording to whom the shawls are given and on what date. Because of privacy issues, it isn't necessary to record the last name of a recipient; a last initial will do. Or you can simply describe the recipient, such as "woman undergoing mastectomy," "man having heart surgery," and so on.

FINALLY, THERE ARE SOME NUTS-AND-BOLTS ISSUES TO ADDRESS (although this is a ministry of the heart and based on prayer) including how yarn and supplies will be acquired and paid for, storage, how shawls will be packaged and presented, how shawls will be transported and delivered, and so on. While these probably don't have to be decided in the first meeting, you'll want your group to find answers to these questions, too.

As this is a prayerful process, remember to begin each gathering, planning meeting, or ministry circle with some ritual, prayer, or blessing. Encourage participants to write their own prayers or write a group prayer that will be included with each shawl given. Some groups begin their gatherings by reading a selection from an inspiration book or scripture and sharing their thoughts on it as they knit.

Every now and then, it's nice to pass someone's shawl-in-progress around the circle. Members can choose to add a few stitches or rows of their own or just hold it quietly, perhaps adding a blessing or wish for the recipient. At the end of your time together, invite members to gather around all the shawls, finished and unfinished, place a hand on them, and recite in unison a prayer or blessing.

As you continue to come together to share thoughts and insights, it will become clearer what direction your particular group will take. Remain open to Divine guidance and don't worry about to whom the shawls will go. The recipients will come to you with ease. Best of all, notice the blessings that flow between the knitter and recipient, and around your faith community, your circle, and your lives.

Contributors

Special thanks to all the knitters and designers who contributed to this book:

RITA GLOD, *Enfield, Connecticut,* who contributed the Original Crocheted Prayer Shawl pattern, page 102.

ROSANN GUZAUCKAS, *Wethersfield, Connecticut,* who partnered with Vicky Cole-Galo to create the Beginner's Shawl pattern, page 82.

SUSAN MEADER TOBIAS, *Washington, DC,* who contributed the Triangle Baptism Shawl pattern, page 100.

JANICE SHULZ, *Heath, Ohio,* who contributed the Pocket Prayer Shawl pattern, page 89. Janice is the founder of the Prayer Shawl Ministry at Christ Evangelical Lutheran Church in Heath, Ohio. In her shawl ministry, a pocket shawl is included whenever a prayer shawl is presented to someone, and one is often given to each member of a family dealing with a major illness or death. The pattern is a wonderful use for yarn leftover from making a large shawl.

KRISTIN SPURKLAND, *Portland, Oregon,* who contributed the Simple Shawl pattern, page 83. Kristin is the author of *Knits from the Heart; Crochet from the Heart; Blankets, Hats, and Booties;* and *The Knitting Man(ual).* When not knitting, among other things, she volunteers at the House of Dreams cat shelter. For more, visit her website www.kristinspurkland.com

MARJORIE WINSTON, *Sellersville, Pennsylvania,* who contributed the Prayer Cloth pattern, page 90. Marjorie created this pattern as slightly larger variety of the pocket prayer shawl. For more information, go to http://sending troopsprayers.bravehost.com

From the Authors

To prayer shawl makers everywhere:
We love these sentiments from two of our friends, and wanted to share them with you.
—Janet and Vicky

"But there is surety in this fiber, weight, strength, and heft on my shoulders, like your hands that wove in triplicate, weaving hope with hope with hope."

—AMANDA BRISTOW

"Women are storytellers, and by sharing our experiences, new insights are created. The richness of making prayer shawls is one way we can interact with people, and it is a gift not to be wasted . . . So pick up your yarn, your knitting needles or crochet hook, and begin an exciting journey through life. Shalom!"

—GLADYS COLE

Yarn Information

We have tried to supply sources below for each of the yarns specified in the patterns in this book. However, you may wish to substitute a yarn that is readily available at your local yarn shop or at retail stores such as Hobby Lobby, Jo-Ann fabric and craft stores, Michael's stores, Target, and Wal-Mart.

If you are substituting brands of yarn, be sure to do a gauge swatch. Yarn companies Bernat, Caron, Lion Brand Yarn, Patons, and Red Heart all offer helpful information on yarn substitution on their websites.

Find Your Local Yarn Shop:

www.sweaterbabe.com/directory
www.knitmap.com
www.yarngroup.org

HOBBY LOBBY
www.hobbylobby.com

JO-ANN FABRIC AND CRAFT STORES
www.joann.com

MICHAEL'S STORES
www.michaels.com

TARGET
www.Target.com

WAL-MART
www.walmart.com

Yarns Used in This Book:

Visit the following websites to find more information on and sources for the yarns used in this book, and other yarns.

LANE BORGOSESIA
Distributed by Trendsetter Yarns
www.trendsetteryarns.com

BERNAT
www.bernat.com

BERROCO
www.berroco.com

CARON
www.caron.com

COLINETTE YARNS
www.colinette.com

DISTRIBUTED BY UNIQUE KOLOURS
www.uniquekolours.com

DECADENT FIBERS
www.decadentfibers.com

ELMORE-PISGAH
www.elmore-pisgah.com

HIFA ULLGARN
www.nordicfiberarts.com

INDEPENDENCE FARM
www.ifalpacas.com

JO-ANN SENSATIONS
www.joann.com

LANA GATTO (WOOL GATTO)
Distributed by Needful Yarns
www.needfulyarnsinc.com

LION BRAND YARN
www.lionbrand.com

**LOUET NORTH
AMERICA**
www.louet.com

MISTI INTERNATIONAL
www.mistialpaca.com

MODA DEA
www.modadea.com

MOUNTAIN COLORS
www.mountaincolors.com

NASHUA HANDKNITS
http://nashuaknits.com/

**DISTRIBUTED BY
WESTMINSTER FIBERS**
www.westminsterfibers.com

PATONS
www.patonsyarns.com

**PLYMOUTH YARN
COMPANY INC.**
www.plymouthyarn.com

ROSARIOS4
www.rosarios4.com

ROWAN
www.knitrowan.com

**DISTRIBUTED BY
WESTMINSTER FIBERS**
www.westminsterfibers.com

SUBLIME
Distributed by Knitting Fever
www.knittingfever.com

TLC
www.coatsandclark.com

Index